The great poets of Italy, in prose and verse; including
a condensation in rhyme of Dante's Divine Comedy,
and a critical introductory review of Italian poets
and poetry from mediaeval to modern times

Thomas Devey Jermyn Farmer, 1265-1321
Divina commedia Dante Alighieri

With the Compliments of

The
Great Poets Of Italy

in Prose and Verse

Including a condensation in Rhyme of
DANTE'S DIVINE COMEDY

and

A Critical Introductory Review of
Italian Poets and Poetry

from

MEDIAEVAL TO MODERN TIMES

BY

Thomas Devey Jermyn Farmer, D.C.L.

TORONTO:
WILLIAM BRIGGS
1916

Bocca baciata non perde ventura anzi
rinuova come fa la luna

Note of Acknowledgment

THE Author has endeavoured in this work to adhere strictly to 'an entire originality of design, arrangement and phraseology, in placing the leading events in the lives of the great Italian authors included and the discussion of their poems before the reader. Of course in a work of this kind one must get more or less of one's actual data and the necessary bare facts and records from former volumes on the same subject, however original he may be in the marshalling of his incidents and the expressing of his ideas. Under this category he has to acknowledge the assistance received from many scholarly articles under different titles in the Eleventh Edition of the Encyclopædia Britannica, from Mr. H. F. Cary's Life and Vision of Dante, from a very instructive and helpful volume by Mr. William Everett entitled "The Italian Poets since Dante," and from Mr. J. H. Wiffen's translation of the " Gerusalemme Liberata" and his "Life of Tasso." The works of two modern women writers on Italian Literature, Florence Trail and Marie L. Egerton Castle, have also been of help in furnishing references and data for the sketches and for the following review.

CONTENTS

ILLUSTRATIONS

PREFACE

SOME time ago the perhaps too ambitious idea suggested itself to me to write "The Lives of the Poets," a cosmopolitan work embracing many names, memoirs and countries. I felt that with our modern and rapid means of communication and transportation, with the vast amount of world travel and interchange of language and ideas between the scholars and literary men and women of the different nations of the Earth occurring to-day (or at least until temporarily arrested by the present great international cataclysm), the poet and the poetical biographer should be able to say with Wesley of old, "The World is my parish." I felt, too, that the only work that claims to-day that all-embracing title, that of the famous Samuel Johnson, in spite of its wit, its scholarship, its many classical allusions and the literary value that it once possessed, has long since been regarded as obsolete as a book of reference and

PREFACE.

is now looked upon more as a relic and a curiosity of the early days of our learning and language than as an authority on even the British poets. But not only was it narrowed down to the British poets alone, it is now universally admitted that the great lexicographer, scholar and man of letters though he undoubtedly was, was too contracted in his ideas and in the scope of his work to embrace at all our very best poets—Chaucer, Ben Jonson, Spenser, Marlowe, Sidney, Shakspeare and other illustrious English names, many of whom only lived a few years before some of those he did include, that he was too bigotted to accord to several of those he touched upon only to damn with faint praise the notice and the fame that they deserved including Gay, Prior, and the gentle Gray, that he was too malignant to do justice to Milton or Swift, and too prone to consign the polished and high-minded Pope to the realms of vulgarity and irreligion. So wanting, too, was the great Doctor in prescience, and in judgment of the literary tastes and requirements of the future, that he had to pad his selection of "lives" with a long panegyric on the virtues of his one-time boon companion in misery, the poor, weak, ill-born, dissolute Savage and to raise to a position among his suggested immortals the names and works of many worse than mediocrities. These have long since been forgotten and would never have been known at all even to the generation after Johnson himself but for the place their famous recorder and apologist gave them in his then wonderful anthology. Others could be mentioned as well, but who ever hears now of Pomfret, Dorset, Stepney, Walsh, Smith, Duke, King, Hughes, Yalden, Hammond, Somerville, or Broome, for each of whom Johnson predicted fame and immortality? Of course due allowance must be made to this famous biographer of the olden times for the many handicaps he laboured under. It must be remembered that he was over seventy years of age when he started on the work which proved him such a false vaticinator. He had not the assistance of the numerous authorities and books of reference that the biographer of to-day enjoys. Our vocabulary then numbered its words in tens where we to-day count them in hundreds and the arts of writing, printing and publishing were heavy and cumbersome in comparison with our own. But a greater obstacle to an impartial and accurate judgment was the fact that Johnson was such an ingrained Tory and High Churchman that his

PREFACE.

very nature prevented him from seeing any patriotism in a Whig or any righteousness in either Romanism or Dissent.

I am aware that many other able scholars since Johnson have given the world encyclopædias, anthologies and biographical groups embracing many famous poets but I have failed to see any of these that treat the subject of poets and poetry from a world standpoint in our own language or from a broader view than that of their own land and countrymen. And so I decided in spite of many personal drawbacks and disadvantages—lack of early literary training and deep classical scholarship, scant knowledge of foreign tongues, only limited travel and research, a mind doubtless warped and grooved by a long professional life, with its best years gone, and other handicaps that could be easily enumerated—to embark on this ponderous work, just because of a love of poetry and the poets, a keen appetite to read and take in, and I hope to remember, all or most of what I have gathered up regarding them in my travels and researches, and that the time to pursue the subject was my own. I realized of course that there were great difficulties in the way of selection, of arrangement, of nationality, of length of the work and of each memoir, and so forth, and that no matter how I succeeded in meeting or overcoming all these, there would at best be many shortcomings, much to criticize, and perhaps a deal to condemn. There were some fundamental principles which I felt I must go by and adopt to start with, if I desired to avoid getting beyond my depth in a sea of impossibility and a maze of difficulty and distraction. One of these was not to attempt to go back to the dim ages of the classic or mythologic past and the mists and conjectures of antiquity. Too abstruse, too scholarly, too unfathomable, too long and tiresome, in fact quite impossible would have been any attempt of mine with my limited time and literary attainments, or, I venture to assert, of any poetical biographer, to include all these in a work of the character I am now outlining. Another rule I laid down was to include no living author however famous—these can wait their turn to be impartially judged when " after life's fitful fever, they sleep well." To include them would not only have made the work too long but also might have raised questions and comparisons better left in abeyance till that great and just arbiter, posterity, can accord to each his merited deserts.

PREFACE.

I also early decided that it would be quite impossible and more than an ordinary life's task for the most facile scholar and writer (attributes which I make no pretense to claim myself) to include memoirs of all the famous poets even of Britain nor more than a very few of the other dominions and nationalities—only specimens as it were or perhaps landmarks of the latter, although I of course intended to select as far as I could, sketches of the best and foremost of each outside country's poets for my work. At the shortest I do not expect to get through with less than a hundred fairly long memoirs and even at that I may be charged with being tedious. Bearing in mind my first-mentioned resolution not to delve too far back into the early vaguenesses and uncertainties of any country's literary history nor behind what we can rely on with reasonable and recorded certainty, I decided that Chaucer should be my starting point with the English poets. He marks the "parting of the ways" as it were between those of our old writers who, on the one hand, continued to write in alternate Latin and French and those who, on the other hand, awakening to a realization of their own country's worth and importance, regarded the English tongue henceforth

14

as " sufficient " in which to crystalize their ideas and write their verse. Likewise when I came to decide upon what I should include in my selection, of those great sources of poetic and literary inspiration to which we owe so much, the Italian poets, though limited to half a dozen or so subjects I had not much difficulty in deciding to begin with Dante. True, I was going back in doing this several generations in time from my English starting-point but the great author of the " Divina Commedia " stands out so pre-eminently as the poetical landmark of his time not only among the poets of Italy but of all other modern civilized lands, that it is only fitting that any work which presumes to deal with the great poets of later Italy must start with him, who, while not the father of all poetry, was unquestionably the father of the second poetic world. True, again, there had arisen among the mediævalists prior to Dante many gifted and polished Italian poets. The Trovatori of Provençe had invaded Italy in the previous century and the Sicilian bards, headed and encouraged by their King Frederick the Second and his gifted son Enzo, had extended their fame into the north as master lyrists and sonneteers and as the authors of some of the most catching love ditties. The Bolognese, Guido Guinicelli, whose song, "The Nature of Love," Longfellow six centuries afterwards so finely translated, may be mentioned as a leader among these pre-Dantean amatory poets. The Florentine, Cavalcanti, also shone lustrously here with his nobility of race, his fine personality, and his uninterrupted flow of scholarly and cultured expression. Dante's own master, Brunetto Latini, also took a high place among these as a composer of allegoric verse, and the Tuscan, Lapo Gianni, had won merited praise in his efforts to adopt in his love songs the native as against the Provençal manner and style. But all these, in spite of their many charms and gifts, may be said to have merely toyed, each in his turn, with the newly-evolved tongue, when we compare their puny efforts with the wonderful and varied outpourings and originality of the master mind, the real creator of the Italian language, with a brief account of whose accomplishments and career I am opening this little volume.

I did not include in this anthology the great Boccaccio because I felt, while admitting that he was undoubtedly a great poet, that we owe to him the "Ottava-rima," one of our own Byron's favourite forms of stanza, that his "Filostrato" and his "Teseide" were adopted by Chaucer as the models for his " Troilus and Creseide" and that from some of his works our great Shakspeare himself took hints for and founded several of his dramas, that notwithstanding all this he and his greatest work " The Decameron," his hundred novels in one, the first specimen we have of modern Italian fiction, more properly come within the scope of a work on prose and prose writers. I think with this omission and explanation I can fairly lay claim to having covered in the work which I here present, a reasonably full though perhaps somewhat superficial review of Italian poets and poetry from the end of the thirteenth to the middle of the nineteenth century. Perhaps I may take the liberty of going a little further than this and of claiming that including my brief reference later on in this article to some modern names not included in this work I have at least dealt with all the great landmarks of Italian verse from the period at which my memoirs begin down to the present erà of contemporary Italian poetry. This will be better understood when I explain that during this apparently long period of time extending over nearly six full centuries, there were three intervals in which both literature and poetry in Italy were in a quiescent, if not in an entirely decadent state. Between Dante and Petrarch Pistoja the exiled lawyer-poet had extolled in beautiful sonnets the virtues of Selvaggio Vergiolese and had also consoled Dante himself on the passing of Beatrice. But between the period of Petrarch and Boccaccio (who were close contemporaries) on the one hand (1304-1375) and that of Ariosto on the other (1474-1533) no brilliant lights had shone in the poetic firmament of Italy. Outside the weak romances of chivalry and the worthy efforts of Lorenzo de Medici (1448-1492) on behalf of both drama and pastoral poetry and in the saving of Italian letters from the deluge of " humanism," no truly valuable addition had been made in that long space of time to her literature. True, Pulci (1431-1490) had figured cleverly in burlesque and, in the Florentine patois in which he wrote, had made light of the religion of his country. Boiardo (1434-1494), the father of romantic poetry, had written and Berni (1490-1535), the satirist, had revised the " Orlando Innamorato." The latter too had fitted the ottava rima to that caustic style in which he wrote and which Byron was afterwards so effectively to adopt in " Don Juan," but nothing more extensive nor more worthy had illumined the lyric page of Italy

18

during this extended interval, although Italian drama had perhaps shared a somewhat better fate.

Then again, after the era of Tasso (1544-1594), occurred another and a much longer period of languor and literary ineptitude, stretching over nearly two hundred years. In this long, dull interval those Italians who followed letters and poetry had to satisfy themselves with the conceits of the Della Cruscans, the artificialities of the Secentismo (Empirics) and the triflings and weak effusions of the Arcadians (Classicists), the languid, puerile efforts of Marini, Guarini, Tassoni, Casti, with an occasional refreshing or enlivening outburst from such artists as Filicaja (1642-1707) and Metastasio (1698-1782). Soon after Tasso Chiabrera had written elegant epitaphs that our own Wordsworth has gracefully translated. Long after him Fortiguerra (1674-1736) philosophized in verse, the priest Frugoni (1692-1768) deluged Italy with his christening, wedding and ordination odes and Varano (1705-1788) imitated the Divine Comedy.* But there was no life nor freshness in any of these stilted outpourings. From this lethargic state the Italian lettered

---

* There are of course other famous, or at least worthy, names beside those I am mentioning here (such as Parini and Goldoni) who helped to bridge over these different hiati in the continuity of Italian literature. These will be found in their chronological order in the proper parts of this volume, and to this extent must be taken like the seven memoirs themselves as incorporated into and forming a part of this review.

world was at length aroused to theatric and poetic life by the original* and powerful tragedies of Alfieri.

Thirdly, after Alfieri's time (1749-1803) and down to the advent of Leopardi (1798-1837) there will not unfortunately be found in Italian poetry any, or at least more than one, great outstanding figure, lyric, epic, romantic or dramatic. Monti (1754-1828), the dramatic imitator of Dante and in turn the panegyrist of both republican and monarchical rulers and institutions, certainly could lay no claim to such a title nor could the Venetian Foscolo (1778-1827), who in later life resided in England, great scholar, romanticist and radical that he was. Manzoni, the Milanese novelist and hymnologist, who lived to as late as 1873, undoubtedly won a high place in his day especially with his ode on the death of Napoleon and as the most brilliant romanticist of the times. Had I sufficient space here to allow me to include another name in my group of the greatest of Italian poets Allesandro Manzoni would surely be my next choice. His tragedies opened up the romantic era in Italian literature and his "Fifth of May" was declared by as great

---

* Original not in conception of design nor invention of plot, but in their severe freshness and in that lack of tedious stateliness and those profuse stage dressings and decorations so common to the average play of the time.

an authority as Goethe to be the finest of modern lyrics. Indeed I long hesitated whether he or Leopardi should form the subject of my seventh and last memoir. It was only the fact that Manzoni's great novel " I Promessi Sposi " (The Betrothed), as in the earlier case of Boccaccio, seems to draw greater attention to him than his poetry, that decided me in favour of the Recanatian. And even this great work of fiction breathes the poetic spirit all through it. In humour, style and loftiness of sentiment it is a poem, though in prose form.

But the fame of the rest was largely local and transient. None of them can be numbered among the immortals. None of them could measure up to the great master minds of former times in bulk or quality nor could they approach in novelty, originality or classical scholarship to that great declamatory satirist and lyrist with whose literary career I have closed this volume—the poor, gloomy, sickly Leopardi. He brings Italian poetry down to nearly the middle of the nineteenth century. I do not, as I have already said, intend to touch here upon any contemporary or living names. But a few of the most noted Italian poets coeval with or subsequent to Leopardi and not already referred to may be briefly mentioned in closing my review. The Tyrolese Prati (1814-1884), who was poet laureate at Turin, had drawn attention to his own province by the spontaneity and boldness of his odes, some of which Mr. Howells has translated, and which like those of his master Manzoni were imbued with a religious vein. Ippolito Pindemonte (1753-1828), revolutionist that he was, like his two famous contemporaries Monti and Foscolo, translated the Odyssey and produced a fine tragedy "Arminius." Others among this band known as "the patriots" were Giambattista Niccolini (1782-1861), who in his unrivalled drama "Arnaldo da Brescia" dealt a blow at Romanism and the papacy, and Silvio Pellico (1788-1854), who acquired fame as a tragedian. It is interesting to note that most of the latter's works were composed in an Austrian prison He wrote altogether twelve tragedies, the first "Francesca da Rimini" being his best. Giuseppe Giusti (1783-1854) also excelled among this group as a satirist. And Italy in the middle of the last century had as well several noted female poets. Caterina Ferrucci of Nardi (1803-1887) united the delicate and the sublime in her Petrarchian canzone entitled "The Flowers and the Stars." Another Caterina, surnamed

PREFACE.

Brenzoni (1813-1856), of Verona exalted the praise of astral splendours and heavenly harmonies in her forceful lyric entitled "The Heavens." But nearly all these writers since Leopardi aimed at popularity and sentimentality only and were gradually again degenerating their country's verse into weakness and artificiality. From this it was fortunately rescued, this time by Giosue Carducci (1836-1907), who, scorning popularity and turning once more to classicism, brought the poetry of Italy back again to that aristocratic intellectuality under which it had always thriven best. But it must be granted that Carducci, great leader in Italian letters that he was, was admired more for his polished speech and ripe learning than for any native spontaneous poetic charm that he possessed.

Having thus completed my survey of the Italian field of poetical biography and gleaned as I passed what I regarded as its richest and best product, having exhausted all the space I felt I could apportion to that part of my larger work and having gotten well advanced with many of the memoirs of our own poets and several more of the foreign ones, I only then began to realize that I had a task ahead of me which to accomplish properly and carefully would involve not months but years. I felt that to do my whole subject justice would take much more time, travel and research than I had at first anticipated, with the possibility, considering the uncertainty of our time here and the length of a work that will, when finished, require several volumes to hold it, of its never being completed at all. And so the idea occurred to me of issuing as a separate work, and under a title of its own, what now appears here, without waiting to finish the larger and more exhaustive undertaking. It will be observed that I have closed the biographical sketches of each subject included in this little volume, as I am also doing with those of the others in my larger work, with some dedicatory thoughts of my own in verse. I trust these trifling poetic efforts, each fitted in a different stanzaic framework and accompanied by a portrait of the subject of the sketch, even if they cannot add any kudos to the mighty names whose lives and works they are intended to very unworthily outline, will at least not detract from their renown and may be of some assistance in the study of the careers of these great masters of Italian verse to whom and to whose country our own poetry owes so much.

And how much it does owe! In the achievements of

PREFACE.

such men as Dante, Petrarch and Boccaccio Italy was
the first of the European nations to herald the dawn of
the Renaissance, to lead in the awakening from that
long mediæval sleep—that mental dungeon in which
humanity had pined before the fourteenth century—
into the consciousness of individual liberty! She it
was who had been the foremost to draw the attention
of mankind from the dark and cloistered pursuits of
the middle ages and by the installation of a more
human literature to impress on them the wealth of
their own minds and the importance of human life
outside and beyond the teachings of the ecclesiastics.
She was the first proclaimer of a new birth to liberty
to the rest of Europe by the creation of a fresh spiritual atmosphere of culture and intellectual freedom
which was destined in future ages to form the very
life-breath of European civilization!

A visit to these glorious old haunts of the great
Italian masters—Florence, Ferrara, Rome, Ravenna,
Pisa, Arqua, Sorrento and the rest—soon brings a realization of how and why, besides the record of her
glorious achievements just related, so many of our own
poets turned towards Italy for their inspiration. There
poetry seems to spring like magic from everything

about one, sky and sea, castle and dungeon, mountain and river, olive grove and vineyard. I have already spoken of the Italian inspiration of Chaucer, Shakspeare and Byron. Surrey and Wyatt, who brought us the sonnet, who perfected our system of versification and corrected our national poetic taste, were the leaders of "those courtly makers who travelled in Italy and there tasted the sweet and stately measures and style of Italian poetry, the novices newly crept out of the schools of Dante, Petrarch and Ariosto." Spenser and Marlowe drank deeply of her life-giving wells of thought. Milton, a century later Gray, and two centuries later Robert Browning, Wordsworth, Scott and Rogers, all returned from Italy with more breadth and culture and tuned to higher flights of poetic effort. Crashaw, Cowley's "divine" protegè, had in England's Commonwealth days sought and found a haven among the cloisters of Italy. She only seemed able to supply that balm which his broken spirit needed, when everything around him—home, country, friends— seemed engulfed in hopeless darkness and despair. The halo of her literature and her song and the charm of her sky and scenery, drew Shelley, Keats, Clough, Landor and Elizabeth Barrett Browning, not only to

26

live but also to die in Italy and the works of all these are redolent with her sweets and her sublimity! Her recent entrance, too, into our great struggle against the threatened world domination of the Teuton, and the heroic part she is taking in that titanic contest for national and individual liberty, must appeal to us all. This in itself alone should help to turn the thought of every modern English-speaking scholar and reader towards an interest in and a study of Italy's glorious past in literature and poetry.

In the work now presented I have ventured to discuss and dwell upon great men, mighty themes, world-moving episodes and the very fountain springs of modern literature. In addition to what the work purports to be—a summary of Italian poets and poetry— I find I have, perhaps unconsciously, blended into it various comments upon and references to many of our English poets and their writings, and have here and there made comparisons between these and their contemporary Italian authors.

Considering the vastness of the field and subject matter invaded my efforts have no doubt been somewhat superficial and cursory and I fear quite inexhaustive. But with the time and space available to me at

PREFACE.

present I realized that I dare not venture deeper into this particular province of the subject, however interesting and instructive its further pursuit might be. My object and desire in producing the present work have been to do so in a scholarly and elevated tone and yet in such simple and concise language and phraseology that even those unversed in the classic can comprehend it. I trust that however unworthy the result as a whole I have at least in a measure accomplished this aim.

T. D. J. F.

"KINGSLOW," OAKVILLE, CANADA,
    October, 1916.

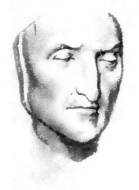

DANTE ALIGHIERI

PART I.

DANTE

DANTE

Dante Alighieri, born in Florence in May, 1265.* Died
at Ravenna, September 14th, 1321.

THIS, admittedly the greatest of Italian, and perhaps
of modern world poets, was born at Florence in May,
1265. In many respects he resembles, in both character and work, the English Milton, who was to follow
him nearly four hundred years afterwards. Like Milton, he came of good family, was scholarly and fond of
music. Like him he felt " the slings and arrows of
outrageous fortune," although he took his discomfiture with a better grace and less austerity of life. In
Dante the adversities of his early and middle life
turned in old age into scorn and invective; in Milton
into grave and desponding melancholy. But, most like
of all to the great Englishman, to Dante was revealed
in a remarkable degree all the mysteries of the spirit
world and the inviolable punishments and rewards

---

* The dates mentioned in the headings of this and the other six
memoirs included are taken from Toracco, who seems as reliable as any
existing literary historian. The exact date of Dante's birth is unknown.
All the others can be assumed with reasonable certainty to be correct.

31

meted out to mankind for the deeds done in the flesh. This marked distinction must be noted, however, that in giving to the world these revelations the two poets adopted entirely different procedures. In Dante's account he is himself the chief actor and narrator; in Milton's he is but the relator of the experience of others.

It would be both wearisome to the reader and out of place in a brief memoir like this to attempt to give an account of the bitter feuds between Guelph and Ghibelline and later between the Whites and the Blacks (Bianchi and Neri) the two factions into which the victorious Guelphs, after subduing their opponents, formed themselves, which divided Florence at the time Dante wrote and which had done so from time to time for fifty years before his birth. Suffice it to say that his participation in the politics and the civil wars of his country, first as a Guelph, then as a White, after the Guelphs had suppressed the Ghibellines, and the attitude of independence if not of open hostility which he assumed to the then-reigning Pope Boniface led to his banishment from his native city, and to his becoming and remaining a wanderer and an exile till his death at Ravenna in 1321. He sprang from the

knightly family of Cacciaguida, and his second or sur-
name of Alighieri also came from a golden wing on
the coat of arms of that family.   Dante's father died
when he was a child.   Of his mother nothing is known.
The learned Brunetto Latini was his teacher and under
him the youth soon acquired a knowledge of polite
literature and all those attainments which were within
reach of the noble Florentines of his day.   It was the
custom of all the educated young men of Dante's
period and country and station in life to write verse,
usually of an amatory nature, and to do so successfully
some affinity or ideal of the opposite sex was selected.
At nine years of age the poet tells us he met Beatrice,
a beautiful young girl, the daughter of one Portinari,
about the same age as himself.   For sixteen years,
although it is said he only actually saw her once or
twice in life and she knew little of him and married
another,* he poured forth a constant stream of worship
and spiritual devotion to this ideal young woman, the
remoteness of the object of his passion only making it
burn the brighter, and after her death he immortalized

---

* Marie Louise Egerton Castle, in discussing Dante, suggests more
frequent meetings than this. She also gives eight as the age when the
child lovers first met and hints that Dante may have actually been at
the wedding of Beatrice and Simone dei Bardi.

her in the Paradise of his "Divina Commedia." In
spite of the great grief he displayed at her passing,
he did not wait long to seek other feminine solace and
married into the Donati family about a year afterwards (1291). It is recorded that this latter union
was marred by the ill-temper of the wife. Possibly
this was occasioned by the Donati being political enemies of the poet and through his consigning their
Chief, Corso, in the "Divina Commedia" to an ignominious place in purgatory. Viewing the case from
a present-day standpoint it is easy to conceive that,
independently of this, most wives would object to being
continually reminded, as Gemma no doubt was, of the
many virtues and excellencies of the departed Beatrice.

Dante had a numerous offspring and two of his sons,
Pietro and Jacopo, were themselves poets. The gift
was evidently further handed down through many generations for we read that as late as the end of the fifteenth century a descendant of this son Pietro, known
as Dante the 3rd, was an elegant poet living in affluence
at Verona and that the Florentines, anxious to make
amends for their ill-treatment of his great ancestor,
besought this representative of the family, but to no
purpose, to come and reside at Florence. His only

daughter, Beatrice, named no doubt after his spiritual affinity, became a nun at Ravenna and it is on record that in her old age the Florentine Republic, as a small amend for the shameful treatment meted out to her father, made her a present through Boccaccio of ten florins of gold.

A few words here descriptive of some of Dante's wanderings and vicissitudes after Florence cast him out may not be out of place. Previously attached to the Guelph faction, he met at Arezzo, Busone da Gubbio, an exiled Ghibelline, a man of letters and versed in Italian poetry. The two became friends and largely through his influence Dante decided now to throw in his lot with his old enemies. From this on he may be ranked as a Ghibelline. But it was only because he saw in his own party no hope of a cure for their petty quarrels and dissensions and that he hoped (though the hope was not in his time at least to be realized) that out of the other party might arise a policy and a leader which would make for a united Italy, that he made the change.

An attack on Florence by the Arezzians having failed, Dante is next found at Padua, then at Mugello at a meeting in the Abbey of Santa Gaudenzio. In

1307 he took refuge with Morello Malaspina in Lunigiana, who, though Dante had formerly been an enemy, received the poet hospitably. Next he is found under the roof of the mighty Lord of Verona, Can Grande, to whom he refers in the XVIIth canto of Paradise as

> "That mortal who was at his birth imprest
> So strongly from his star that of his deeds
> The nations shall take note."

About this time Henry of Luxemburg became Emperor and Dante seems to have pinned his faith to him as the deliverer of his country. From his former attitude as a suppliant he appears now to have assumed a defiant tone towards Florence and called on the new monarch to crush the usurping rulers of his native city. But Henry was weak and vacillating; he died without accomplishing anything, so that little but disappointment came to Dante of these bright hopes of delivery and reinstatement. He journeyed to Paris and the Low Countries. Some authorities say he went as far as Germany and even to England. There are records extant that he visited Porciano Castle in the valley of the Casentino, that he took temporary refuge in the Urbinian Mountains and that in

DANTE.

a wild and lofty Avellanian monastery he composed about this time a large part of his " Divine Comedy." His former Arezzian friend, Busone da Gubbio, also now entertained the homeless poet in the Castle of Colmollaro. Udive and the Friuli also lay claim to his having sojourned and written in both these places. His last refuge was with the poet Polenta at Ravenna:

> " Situate on the coast where Po descends
> To rest in Ocean with his sequent streams "

where, having lived three years and becoming heart-broken over the failure of an expedition on which his patron had sent him to Venice, Dante sickened and died in either July or September, 1321.

Dante was noted for his eloquence, and this gift may in a measure be said to have brought about his death almost in the prime of life. The flourishing Venetians were about to declare war on Ravenna and Guido da Polenta, his host, knew of no one more fluent in oratory to plead his cause before the warlike Doge, hence the selection of Dante for the task which ended so disastrously for the poet. His funeral was an imposing one. His body, adorned with all the trappings of poetry, was borne on a funeral car accompanied by the leading citizens through the principal streets of Ravenna and laid in a marble coffin over which the Lord of Ravenna himself pronounced the funeral oration. Many epitaphs were called forth by the demise of the great poet-exile; the best of them composed by his friend Giovanni di Virgilio. Florence had in 1316 made overtures to the outcast to return but they contained humiliating conditions which Dante would not consider. After his death, realizing what they had lost, the Florentines made frantic but vain efforts to have his remains brought home. A monument to him was erected in his native city in the Church of Santa Croce early last century but his bones still rest at Ravenna in the sepulchre begun by Polenta and finished at the close of the fifteenth century by the father of Cardinal Bempo. Cardinal Gonzaga also caused a further and a most costly memorial to be erected to the great poet, also at Ravenna, in 1780.

Boccaccio tells us that Dante was a man of middle stature, of solemn demeanour and slow walk, that he usually dressed well, that he had a long face, an aquiline nose, full eyes, large cheek bones, and a projecting upper lip; that his complexion was olive and his hair and beard thick and curled; in short, that his appearance was so singular as to call forth the taunt from his enemies that he resembled an inhabitant of that hell to which he was prone to consign so many of them.

Dante's chief work is of course his "Divina Commedia," but why he should assign to a literary production which is really a satirical epic the very contradictory title of "Comedy" it is hard to conceive and has never been explained. One writer* suggests that it was because it began sadly and ended happily, and further that its author regarded Virgil as the tragedian *par excellence*. The title "Divine" was of course affixed afterwards by Dante's compatriots. He began the task when about thirty-eight years old and when, after becoming satiated with military and civil affairs and with those ordinary efforts in both prose and poetry which most educated men of his day dallied with, he had experienced what may be termed a conversion of soul to higher and better aspirations in life. He had completed only seven cantos of the "Inferno" when his banishment took place. It is not likely, with all the trials and vicissitudes which followed, that the work would ever have been continued had not one of

---

* Florence Trail.

his protectors in exile, Malaspina, gotten hold of the abandoned fragment and, recognizing its worth, urged his poet-guest to go on with the task begun under conditions so much more promising. There is no evidence as to how and where he finished it, but there is no doubt that the rest of the " Divina Commedia " was accomplished under almost inconceivable difficulties and adverse circumstances. The last two books, " Purgatory " and " Paradise," certainly show a falling off and a taming and softening of the wild and gloomy imagination of the writer as depicted in his " Inferno," for which he seems to have taken the descent of Aeneas for his model. In perusing the whole work one can readily see, after passing on from the " Inferno," that the incentive to high literary effort, especially marked at the outset of his task, appears as the end draws nearer to become less pronounced. As an evidence of how the feeling of the Florentines towards Dante had turned in one or two generations from contempt and hatred to reverence, it may here be mentioned that in 1373 a public allowance was made to lecturers on Dante's great work. Boccaccio was the first of these. Petrarch was also one of six learned Italians selected by the Archbishop of Milan in 1350 to write a com-

DANTE.

mentary on the "Divina Commedia." Lecturers on Dante's works were also appointed by other Italian cities, among them Pisa, Bologna and Venice. Indeed this revulsion in sentiment may be said to have come much earlier than I have mentioned, for it is recorded that a celebrated physician, Ceno de Ascoli, was burned at the stake only three years after the poet's death for maligning Dante in some parodies on the latter's verse. Nor is it to be wondered at that this great work should have excited the curiosity and the deep personal interest of succeeding generations of Florentines when the incidents recorded in it came so nearly home to so many noted citizens. With the various places of torture, of trial, or of bliss, in the spirit world assigned to so many well-known characters, from sovereign or lord, pope or cardinal, down to the ordinary citizen, there could hardly have been a resident of any repute in Florence who had not some relative or friend, or at least some person great or small, in whom he had an interest depicted to advantage or misfortune (usually the latter) in Dante's weird but realistic narrative.

It will not, I trust, be out of place to outline here a brief account of the great Florentine poet's wonderful journey, and the thrilling experiences he met with, as

he passed through those three divisions into which the
Ancient Church to which he belonged at that time
separated, and still apportions man's future state,
though in doing so I will be running the risk of making
this sketch of Dante somewhat longer than the others
included in the present volume. Beginning with his
straying from the beaten path in a dense forest which
the poet means to typify as the Cares of the World,
and his hindrance from escape by the three wild
beasts of pleasure, pride and avarice, it tells of his
meeting with Virgil. The latter is supposed to personify philosophy, and to have been urged by Beatrice
to go to the lost poet's assistance. Dante is led by
him first through hell, a vast conical-shaped hollow
reaching to the centre of the earth. This huge vortex
is separated into three divisions for the reception and
punishment of the incontinent, the brutish and mal-
icious. The punishments are apparently on a graded
scale of which the last are the most terrible, loathsome
and ignominious. He first witnesses the fate of the
apathetic, the unbaptized, the carnally minded, the
gluttonous, the prodigal and the arrogant. They then
enter the City of Dis or Hades where heretics are
confined in red-hot tombs and next descend to where

those who have done violence to their neighbours are deluged in a river of blood. Here, too, suicides are converted into rude trees upon which harpies build their nests or are torn by female mastiffs, and those guilty of blasphemy and other like offences are tormented by continual showers of fire flakes:

"O'er all the sand fell slowly, wafting down
Dilated flakes of fire as flakes of snow
On Alpine summit when the wind is hushed."

A little further on they encounter Brunetto Latini, Dante's old teacher, condemned for usury, and next, those who have not in life respected woman's chastity, whose punishment is to be scourged by demons, and then the flatterers, who are immersed in filth. Those guilty of simony, including Pope Nicholas V, are now encountered fixed head-downward, their feet tortured with fire. Fortune tellers and astrologers are next met with their heads set face backwards so that they cannot see to walk, and the embezzlers of public funds are engulfed in boiling pitch. They then witness the hypocrites being borne down with the weight of leaden caps, mockingly lined on the outside with gold and pacing round the sixth gulf. In the seventh they be-

hold robbers tormented by serpents; in the eighth evil
counsellors enveloped in flames. In the ninth are met
the scandal mongers and those guilty of heresy and
schism, who are punished by the maiming of their
limbs; and in the tenth, or last gulf of this the eighth
circle, called Malebolge, they hear the pitiful cries of
those condemned to eternal leprosy, the alchemist, the
forger, the counterfeiter and the false pretender. In
Cocytus, the ninth, or frozen circle, the last which the
poet and his guide visit, and the most inaccessible and
horrible of all the places of torment, are confined the
traitors, and here, though his heart is hardened against
the other sufferers, Dante pathetically tells the story
of Ugolino whom he meets and who, adjudged guilty
of treachery, was with his innocent sons and grand-
sons starved to death in a tower by the Pisans at the
instigation of Archbishop Ruggieri. The poet in passing calls down a curse on the town for its barbarous
treatment of those innocent of the crime, in these
scathing words:

> " O thou Pisa, shame
> Of all the people who their dwelling make
> In that fair region where the Italian voice
> Is heard, since that thy neighbours are so slack

DANTE.

To punish, from their deep foundations rise
Capraria and Gorgona and dam up
The mouth of Arno that each soul in thee
May perish in the waters. What if fame
Reported that thy castles were betrayed
By Ugolino? yet no right hadst thou
To stretch his children on the rack, for them,
Brigata, Uguccione and the pair
Of gentle ones of whom my song hath told,
Their tender years, thou modern Thebes, did make
Uncapable of guilt."

Here he also sees Lucifer punishing in his triple pair
of bloody jaws Judas, the arch betrayer of his Lord
and Master, and Brutus and Cassius, the two other
greatest traitors of the world.

Relieved from the foul air that surrounds the lower
depths, they now emerge in the grey dawn of Easter,
into the purer atmosphere of that region:

" In which the human soul from sinful blot
Is purged and for ascent to heaven prepared."

Purgatory is described by Dante as being near the
summit of a mountain which the two poets ascend by
a steep path. On the way up they meet some souls

who are condemned to linger where the travellers see them because they repented too late in life, also Sordello, the great twelfth century Mantuan poet, who leads them into a flowery valley where are the spirits of many-crowned heads, hoping for, but not yet entitled, to final and eternal bliss. Dante is then carried sleeping by Saint Lucy to the very gates of Purgatory, where he again finds Virgil waiting for him and both then enter. Purgatory proper is depicted as divided into seven ledges or cornices, upon the first five of which rest the souls of those who are being cleansed of the sins of pride, envy, anger, indifference and avarice. On the fifth cornice they are joined by Statius, the post-Augustan Epic poet of the first century and author of Thebais, and all three ascend to the sixth where the sin of gluttony is purged and where Forese declaims against the immodesty in dress of the Florentine ladies. They then pass up to the seventh cornice or ledge where unfaithful husbands and wives are given, through purging fire, an opportunity of repentance. Dante himself is also forced to submit to the heat of this cleansing fire. The last ascent is now reached, which leads to the terrestrial paradise. Here Virgil leaves Dante to be his own guide:

DANTE.

> " Both fires, my son,
> The temporal and eternal, thou hast seen
> And art arrived where of itself my ken
> No further reaches. I, with skill and art
> Thus far have drawn thee, now thy pleasure take
> For guide."

The latter wanders on through the forest of this terrestrial paradise and comes to a stream, on the opposite side of which he sees a fair lady culling flowers.
Both walk up the stream, a narrow one:

> " By the stream
> Three paces only were we sunder'd."

each on their own side and the lady, who in life was
Duchess of Tuscany, but is now Matilda, the personification of affection for the Church, explains to Dante
that the waters which divide them are those of Lethe:

> " With power
> To take away remembrance of offence."

The apocalyptic things spoken of in Ezekiel and the
revelation of St. John are now revealed to the bewild-
ered traveller and a dazzling and majestic car appears,
drawn by a gryphon, the latter typical, in its union of
the eagle and the lion, of the Saviour of Mankind.

47

THE GREAT POETS OF ITALY.

"So beautiful
A car in Rome ne'er graced Augustus pomp
Or Africanus'. E'en the Sun itself
Were poor to this."

Among the attendants on the car are the three graces
and the four cardinal virtues, all in the form of
nymphs or virgins, and also figures representing
Moses, St. John, St. Luke, St. Paul and the authors
of the New Testament epistles. Beatrice, symbolical
of revealed religion, now descends from heaven in a
cloud of flowers and stands alongside the gryphon.
She speaks to Dante from the other side of the stream,
rebuking him for his worldliness. Then Matilda, his
former fair fellow-traveller seizes him, fallen pros-
trate from the effect of Beatrice's rebuke, and drawing
him through the water, presents him to the four
nymphs, Prudence, Justice, Fortitude and Temperance, who in turn lead him to the gryphon and Beatrice. The three other virgins, Faith, Hope and
Charity, then intercede with Beatrice to shew the poet
her second beauty. All then pass on to a high tree
supposed to represent the Roman Empire and whose
higher branches spread wider than the lower, contrary
to the natural order of trees. Under this tree the

beautiful car drawn by the gryphon and supposed to symbolize the Christian Church, is struck by a shaft from Jove representing persecution, sprung upon by a hungry fox meaning heresy, feathered by an eagle which symbolizes the gifts of Constantine to the Church, and torn asunder by a dragon representing Mahomet. A vaunting harlot seated on an eminence nearby, accompanied by a giant, is also portrayed, supposedly to show forth respectively the baneful influence on the Church of Pope Boniface VIII and Philip the Fourth of France. Lastly the whole procession moving on arrives at the fountain from which spring both the waters of Lethe and those of Eunoe, a stream flowing in the opposite direction, the latter imbued with power:

> "To bring
> Remembrance back of every good deed done."

Thither Dante and Statius are led by Matilda at the request of Beatrice, and drinking, the poet returns:

> "From the most holy wave regenerate
> E'en as new plants renewed with foliage new
> Pure and made apt for mounting to the stars."

The last part of this wonderful vision deals with heaven and the rewards of the blessed who inhabit it.

THE GREAT POETS OF ITALY.

With Beatrice, the poet ascends from purgatory, first
to the moon, then to Mercury, Venus, the Sun, Mars,
Jupiter, Saturn and the fixed stars, which are respectively the different heavens numbered from the first
to the eighth. In all these Dante meets and converses
with the redeemed spirits of many famous persons,
Kings, Saints, Martyrs, prophets and patriarchs.
Among them he mentions the Empress Constanza, the
Emperor Justinian, Charles Martel, Thomas Aquinas,
King Solomon, his own ancestor Cacciaguida and St.
Benedict and he is even permitted to view the Christ
and His Divine Mother. They then ascend into the
ninth or last heaven, the " Primum Mobile," where all
motion and time have their roots and where:

> " Except the Soul Divine
> Place in this heaven is none. The soul divine
> Wherein the love that ruleth o'er its orb
> Is kindled, and the virtue that it sheds—"

Here the poet is permitted to behold the divine essence
and then he and Beatrice ascend further still to the
Empyrean from whence they witness the final triumph
of the souls of the blest. This is pictured as an immense white rose where myriad souls of the redeemed
like innumerable swarms of bees sing and disport in

DANTE.

joy amid the heavenly fragrance. Beatrice now leaves Dante and returns to her throne and St. Bernard takes her place at the poet's side. He shows him the souls of the saints of both the old and new testaments on their thrones and prays to the Virgin to give Dante grace to contemplate the brightness of Divine Majesty. Dante prays for ability to show forth the Celestial Glory in his verse and finally is given a glimpse of the Trinity and the power to comprehend all mysteries:

> "With fixed heed, suspense and motionless,
> Wondering I gazed; and admiration still
> Was kindled as I gazed. It may not be,
> That one, who looks upon that light, can turn
> To other object, willingly, his view.
> For all the good that will may covet, there
> Is summ'd; and all, elsewhere defective found,
> Complete."

(I have taken this and my other quotations from the translation by Mr. Cary.) Dante also vividly relates many other experiences he encounters during this the third and last and, of course, the calmest and happiest portion of his spiritual journey. The different redeemed souls the poet meets tell of the various tests they have passed through and of the trials they have

51

endured, some of reparation made for broken vows of chastity, others of their martyrdom for the true faith; others again arranged in the figure of a majestic eagle, take credit for their pure administration of justice while on earth.

The warriors from the crusades relate their deeds of valour in endeavouring to rescue the Saviour's tomb, while a still further assemblage tell of holy lives spent in retirement and contemplation. Adam, the great parent of mankind, relates to Dante his experiences during the Creation and the fall, when he arrived in heaven, and the language he spoke on earth. Our traveller also has some doubts removed and explained regarding the pardoning of broken vows, human redemption and the salvation of those who had not the opportunity of knowing and therefore could not believe in Christ. He hears the papal power and the clergy roundly condemned for neglect of true religion, for avarice and luxury, and the monks for their corrupt lives. The Florentines are pilloried too, for their present debasement and degeneracy, brought about chiefly, so Dante is informed by his ancestor Cacciaguida, through their co-mingling with inferior neighbouring races. He is told of the futility to save

DANTE.

of mere professions of belief in Christ, and warned against presuming to fathom God's ways. His faith is tested and approved of by Saint Peter, who at the same time bitterly denounces the grasping propensities of his successors on the papal throne. St. James questions the poetic wayfarer on Hope; St. John on Charity, and Beatrice herself on their journey denounces the perverseness of man and the ignorance and avarice of the theologians and the preachers.

Dante selected the terza rima for his great work and was the first to introduce this stanza, at least artistically, into Italian poetry. This is the form Mrs. Browning uses in her " Casa Guida Windows." Shelley, too, five hundred years after Dante, also on Florentine soil, employed this form in which to crystalize those sadly-exquisite thoughts which came to him when, wandering through Cascini's Wood, near the junction of the tiny Mugnone with the nobler Arno, he gathered from the sporting of the approaching storm with the dead Autumn leaves hurrying by him the inspiration for his unsurpassed " Ode to the West Wind." It may seem strange that this form of verse, so adapted as it is to sparkling epigram, to sustained narrative, to minute description, to biting satire, and to the actual portrayal of every beauty in both art and nature, did not long remain a favourite channel of poetic expression with the Italian poets who followed Dante. It seems to have been almost abandoned after Boccaccio used it. This was owing no doubt to the fact that it requires continued unity of thought, and that it does not permit any break-off without the dropping of a rhyme. Nor can it be said to have ever become popular for the same reasons with the poets of other countries, although we frequently find the Germans experimenting with it. And it will be observed that even Shelley, in the great Ode above mentioned, in order to terminate his five stanzas without destroying his rhyme, departs from the strict Dantean or ternary form and changes the two lines with which he completes each stanza into a couplet.

While the remaining works of Dante are insignificant in comparison with his greatest effort, they are, nevertheless, worthy of high praise. His Vita Nuova, written in Italian, which language he preferred to the Latin and used in most of his works, also overflows with the history and praises of Beatrice and the youthful ardour of its author for his ideal of young womanhood. Although written mostly in prose, it is inter-

spersed with sonnets, ballads and canzoni, teeming
with tenderness and passion. This work was written
in youth, while his Convito or Banquet, a prose theme
composed in a philosophic vein, was produced in later
life. The latter was never actually completed owing
to the poet's comparatively early death but was intended as a sort of note book or running commentary
on the "Divina Commedia" and the other works he had
by this time completed and given to the world. Dante
also wrote some Latin Eclogues and in the same
tongue some learned and valuable prose productions,
but his efforts in the Ancient classic language are
admittedly inferior to his works in his own vernacular.

Dante was a man of varied attainments. In addition to the gifts of poetry and music, he was apt as a
delineator in pencil. He was a hater of flattery, often
prone to sarcasm and although usually sedate and
sombre, could, when the occasion warranted it, rise to
sport and pleasantry. His enemies accused him of
plagiarism, of copying the " Vision of Alberico " in his
"Divina Commedia," a charge that has been hurled at
the best and greatest of poets in all ages. But there was
little ground for this, as almost every country in
Dante's time had its writer on the spiritual and the
supernatural and other origins, besides the thrillingly

weird story of the young nobleman of Alvito might just as easily have been suggested for a skeleton for Dante's tale. It is in reality very little distinguished from what one reads and hears to-day as the experience of the modern spiritualist. It was not the bare idea of the journey through the spirit world and the encounters and experiences there with the various spirit characters and persons mentioned that gives the poet his great name and fame as a portrayer of the weird and the ghostly and the future rewards and punishments of mankind. Many writers before and after him have written upon the same subject and along the same lines of thought but their names and their works are forgotten or at least little known. It is not the conceptions themselves in Dante's journey nor the bare incidents he relates as he tells of his wonderful passage through the realms of spirit land that attract the attention and excite the admiration of the reader. It is the rich word painting, the choice imagery employed, the magnificent verbal clothing with which he adorns his characters and incidents and all the minute and varied details he enters into, which entitle Dante to be ranked among the greatest of imaginative writers of all time.

DANTE.

TO DANTE.

I.

Dante! whose deep, far-reaching mind combines
The rarest gifts of all the Florentines;
Scholar and patriot, greatest far among
Their votaries of satire and of song,
Who of thy fellow countrymen didst tell
The future joy or doom inviolable,
Who of thy fair, soon-sainted Beatrice
Didst paint in words the apotheosis.
Great Cacciaguidan! while I dwell on thee,
I, other bards beholding do but dimly see.

II.

When for deceit at Ponte Vecchio's Gate
Buondelmonte met the traitor's fate,
There rose in Florence strife internecine,
The deadly feuds of Guelph and Ghibelline.
Full fifty years before thou saw'st the light
These savage rivals waged their tireless fight,
Which, like a wind-fann'd flame, increasing more,
Drove thee from love and poetry to war,
Deprived thee of thy family, rank and hearth,
And made of thee a wanderer o'er a friendless earth.

THE GREAT POETS OF ITALY.

III.

From thy Arezzian hiding-place sore press'd
Thou cam'st to Padua, Papafavi's guest,
And in Mugello's sacred precincts found
For a brief period a trysting ground.
At Lunigiana to thee came the proof
Of kind Morello's friendship 'neath that roof
Where white Carrara's marble peaks descend
And with the foam of Spezzia's billows blend.
And now the Castle of the famed Can Grande
A sanctuary gives to thee in far Verona's land.

IV.

Where the swift Arno, goodly river springs
And Porciano spreads her sheltering wings,
Where Faggiola's turrets proudly rise
Amid Urbino's peaks to greet the skies,
The purlieus of Bologna's learned halls,
The Netherlands and Paris' classic walls,
With Gubbio 'neath Colmollaro's towers,
At Lucca too, thou mused away the hours.
Weird Avellana boasts thy monkish cell.
Each gave the exile shelter, none a place to dwell.

DANTE.

V.

But though a wanderer, well hast thou unfurl'd
The hidden mysteries of the spirit world.
How real, how impressive dost thou tell
The tortures of a never-ending hell,
The toils of those whose only hope of glory
Must lead through lingering, cleansing, purgatory.
Unending joy where heavens' summits rise
Where hallowed Beatrice dwells in Paradise.
What an unmatched, unchallenged journey this!
From Dis's mingled torments to the realms of bliss.

VI.

What fates are here! what prophecies abound!
What allegories subtle and profound!
What scorn and praise and pity! what despair!
What destinies of bad and good laid bare!
What knowledge in its varied paths displayed!
Events and persons accurately arrayed!
How cruel falls the stroke of satire's lash!
How anger and contempt reveal and flash!
What forms and features vividly expressed
Of those who wail below or hymn their heavenly rest!

THE GREAT POETS OF ITALY.

VII.

O mighty master of Italian verse,
Deep-branded with the outlaw's cruel curse!
Few were the years that passed ere Florence wept,
Her poet dead, whom others loved and kept.
Ravenna gave at length a home, thy grave
Where leads Corsini to the Adrian wave.
Thy name hangs on each learned tongue to-day,
The brightest name in all that bright array.
And suppliant Florence, though denied thy bier,
Tells proudly to the World that " Dante once lived
      here."

PART II.

PETRARCH

PETRARCH

Francesco Petrarca, born at Arezzo, July 20th, 1304. Died at Arqua, July 18th, 1374.

ABOUT a generation before the father of English poetry saw the light in London, there was born at Arezzo in Tuscany the man who was destined to be the reviver of learning in Italy, and one of her greatest poets. Not only was he to fix the rules for that popular form of verse now known to us as the sonnet, but he was to incorporate it into the very life and genius of Italian poetry. He was, also, on a wider canvas, with a larger theme, a bolder imagination, and a richer fancy than the fettered form of the sonnet could allow, though in just as artful and complicated a system of rhyme, to give expression in his odes, breathing a lover's devotion to his Laura, of utterance at once the most beautiful and thrilling, as well as the most noble and sublime, as had ever before or since adorned Italian verse. He it was who was to establish in a language as perfect and mellifluous to-day as in his own time, the words, the phrases and the tone of Italian poetry, to give to it that melody of expression, that sweetness and tenderness which, like the poetry of Homer of old, makes it adapt itself to music far more readily than does the modern poetry of any other country. To him were his countrymen to look up as their model of thought, of culture, of elegance and also of style. To him it was to be given to receive the poet's crown on that ancient Roman Capitol which ages before had witnessed the coronations of the Scipios and the Cæsars, marking, as he did, the great divide between ancient and modern thought, the old school of literature and poetry and the renaissance. For while his illustrious predecessor Dante chose Virgil for his guide, and bowed to the influence of the latter's poetry, thus leaning towards the old school of thought, Petrarch from the first assumed that contempt for the Latin tongue which was to mark all the followers of the early Italian renaissance. It is true he wrote in Latin as well as Italian, including a long epic entitled " Africa," but he never aspired to or attained in the Latin tongue that mastery of diction and measure of which he came to be such a model in the Italian.

PETRARCH.

The father of Francesco Petrarca was a Florentine notary who had sided with the Ghibbelines and, on the triumph of the Guelphs in 1302 was ejected from Florence by the same decree which sent the great Dante into banishment. Francesco Petrarca was, therefore, born in exile, and he may well be said to have been expatriate for the better part of his whole life, though his last twenty years was spent intermittently between Milan and other towns of northern Italy.

It was an age in which Italy, though advancing rapidly in art and literature and science, was torn by both rival factions from within, and the dread of foreign conquest from without, and no ruler, spiritual or temporal, seemed able to afford any relief. It was little to be wondered at, therefore, that amid the distractions and conflicts of Rome, the Church should heed the call which came to her from Philip the Fair of France, to move the papal seat for the time being at least, from the Eternal City to Avignon, the beautiful and classic capital of Provençe. . Hither, to share in the security and tranquility promised to the Church, came also the head of the Petrarch family with his promising son, shortly after the education of the latter had begun at

Pisa. Here, far removed from the bitter factions and the provincial wrangles of their own country, father and son could survey the situation at home from a less prejudiced point of view than if they were actually participators in the struggle.

At the age of twenty Petrarch lost his father and the youth, having in the meantime passed through the universities of Montpelier and Bologna, returned to Avignon, having also lost his patrimony through the dishonest management of its curator. His charm of manner and breeding, as well as his superior education, seem to have made him a favourite at the papal court from the first, especially with the two famous brothers Colonna, whose influence was willingly offered, and would, no doubt, have pushed the bright young Avignon student to the front in any profession he had seen fit to choose.

Before the age of fifteen Petrarch had studied the humanities, in which he was afterwards to become so conspicuous, but he now followed his father's wishes in taking up the law, then the most honourable and lucrative of the professions, and more or less indissolubly associated with the church. The boy, however, had no taste for the law, and an ardent love for the

PETRARCH.

classic authors and the struggle between his natural desires and obedience to the will of his parent caused him many restless hours. It was but another example of those numerous cases, not only in Italy, but in other lands, where parental ambition towards the learned professions has almost succeeded in depriving literature of its brightest stars. The story has often been told, but will, I hope, bear repetition, of how the elder Petrarch, indignant one day at his son's neglect of his legal studies for literature, angrily gathered together and consigned to the flames every classical author in the house. Finally, however, yielding to the boy's paroxysms of grief, he allowed him to rescue the scorched volumes of Virgil and Cicero from destruction. But the death of his father put an end to all disputation, and left the son, poor though he then found himself in worldly things, to follow his own inclinations.

It is on record that, on first finding himself bereft of all his worldly possessions, he took orders and became a priest, nominally at least. He was offered ecclesiastical preferment more than once, but these opportunities he did not take advantage of, for Petrarch had decided by now that letters and scholarship were to be his avocation in life, and that neither the dry technicalities and quibbles of the law, nor the irksome and monastic duties of the priesthood, were to draw him from his chosen calling. Up to this time there is no evidence of the young scholar's devotion to or even inclination towards poetry, and the reader naturally asks how and when did the immortal spark descend that was to point out Francesco Petrarca as Italy's foremost poet of his time? The answer is wrapped up in the individuality of a woman, beautiful young Laura de Noves, whom the future poet one day saw in church at Avignon, when twenty-three years of age, and whom from the first time he beheld her he allowed to be the inspiration and dominating influence of his whole after life. The passion was not reciprocated, nor is it recorded that the two ever became close acquaintances, but this did not lessen the young poet's respectful ardour for the object of his spiritual devotion, and to her, his ideal of perfect womanhood, from his retirement among the hills and valleys of the Sorgnès, whither he went when he found it was hopeless to expect any return of his love, he poured forth his devotion in sonnet and in song. In our time such a procedure, no matter how eloquent the song, how sublime the sentiment, or how choice the expression, would no doubt cover its author, and the object of his adoration as well, with unenviable publicity and perhaps ridicule. It is not recorded that the apotheosized lady or her friends ever objected to Petrarch's attentions, and his impassioned efforts, his new song of real individual love, rather than bring stricture or ridicule upon his own head, appears to have so dazzled the Italians both high and low, that he was universally acclaimed as worthy of the laureate's crown. Hark to how he describes the object of his love, in one of his many adoring, if somewhat alliterative, passages:

> " Graceful she moved with more than mortal mien,
>   In form an angel, and her accents won
>   Upon the ear with more than human sound.
>   A spirit heavenly, pure, a living sun
>   Was what I saw, and if no more 'twere seen,
>   To unbend the bow will never heal the wound."

He seems to have contented himself to neglect all other pursuits and uninterruptedly sing his lady's praises, even though he won no love or even personal gratitude in return. The writer knows of no instance in the annals of poetry where an author has so completely

devoted his undivided talents, and all the soul and passion of his life, to one especial object, and as far as
we know one quite indifferent to his fervid attentions.
For, outside of his worship of Laura de Noves, with
the exception of a few patriotic odes setting forth the
hopes and sufferings of his beautiful but ill-starred
country, his spasmodic endeavours to arouse her slothful and avaricious rulers to a sense of their duty, and
what some consider his masterpiece in the form of an
allegorical poem setting forth the triumphs of Love,
Chastity, Death, Fame, Time and God, Petrarch may
be said to have written no verse worthy of mention.
Different and entirely opposite versions of his relations
with this ravishingly delightful young woman have
been left us by students of the great Italian poet
whose life and works I am now briefly reviewing.
Although as many as twenty-five different scholars
and biographers have written the life of Petrarch, all
unite at least in conceding to her, or more properly
speaking to the great volume of beautiful verse he
dedicated to her, known as his "Canzoniere," the
poet's title to permanent fame. This, they tell us,
coupled of course with his scholarly and successful
efforts to revive the learning of his time and country,

PETRARCH.

has made the name of Petrarch immortal, not only in Italy, but in the whole lettered world, not his learned Latin treatises, his many triumphs in the fields of politics, travel and philosophy, or his success as a theologian or a diplomat. But how differently do some of these approach the subject of Petrarch's adoration! Lord Woodhouslee denies that Laura was ever married, and contends that up to the day of her death it was Petrarch's intention, if he could, to make her his wife. This learned writer, in support of his contention, refers to the absence in all Petrarch's poetry of any reference to her nuptial state, and to its tenor pointing all the other way. On the other hand, M. de Sade, writing towards the end of the eighteenth century, credits Laura with being the wife of one of his ancestors, Hugh by name, and the mother of eleven children. Again a third class of critics, among whom is Gibbon, argue that Laura had no real existence, that the poet's love was metaphysical only, and its object merely a " shadowy nymph," or in other words, a myth. This much may be said in support of this last contention, that all his written adoration of Laura is more general than individual. He never refers to any of her own special beauties of person or character, and what he says of her might well be said by any ardent poetic lover of the lady of his heart.

But Petrarch's life was in many other respects an active one. He was always ambitious of personal glory and craved the highest honours in the gift of his country and its rulers. Called more than once from his mountain seclusion by those in power who had heard of and desired to use his great talents and scholarship, he was often the chosen mediator between many warring States and princes, and even acted the part of Italian envoy at foreign courts. He took part in the new crusade of Pope John XXIInd, and with the approval of his sovereign, King Robert of Naples, went to Rome, was drawn in state through the Forum, and crowned by the senate of the Eternal City. After his return to Vaucluse from this glorious literary triumph he frequently visited Italy again in his endeavours to inspire those in authority to do something to alleviate his distracted country and bring about union among the striving factions. It was about this time that Petrarch produced those patriotic odes to Colonna, to Rienzi, and to the princes of Italy, whose wonderful declamatory harmony and lofty appeals to the spirit of Italian nationality, proved that their author was,

on occasion, capable of rising to something more substantial than ideal and abstract love ditties.

Boccaccio, a generation younger than Petrarch, and
inclined in his early life to profligacy and frivolity,
sought and valued the friendship of the elder man,
became steadied by his example, and learned from his
erudition and his mastery of letters. The younger
poet, influential at Florence, brought to Petrarch an
offer of restoration to the rights of citizenship and the
rectorship of the newly-founded Florentine University,
but the latter, preferring literary leisure, declined the
generous offer. Tyrants as well as liberators sought
after and were jealous of his good offices, and it is
regretfully to be recorded of Petrarch that, in spite of
his frequent and continued outbursts on behalf of freedom, so great was his pride and his love of self-glori-
fication and stately aggrandizement, that he allowed
himself to become the ally of the worst tyrants of
his day.

In 1341 he had visited Parma as the guest of the
tyrant Azzo di Correggio, who was then installing himself as lord, after driving out the Scaligers, his former
masters. Petrarch, always restless and dissatisfied, had
tired of the monotony of Vaucluse, and decided to

make his home for the future alternately between its romantic haunts and the glitter of court life at Parma. This he did until after the death of Laura and most of the friends of his early life.

About 1353 he abandoned both Parma and Vaucluse and settled at Milan under the patronage of the Viscontis, who had, long before this, acquired as well the Correggian sovereignty over the Parmese. Here, he not only interested himself in the matrimonial alliances of the Viscontis, lent his subtle persuasions to advance their cause with rival houses, and acted for them at the courts of France and Germany, and as arbitrator between Venice and Genoa, but also openly sympathized with and participated in many of their crimes and atrocities. Nor, in spite of the apparent spirituality of his devotion to Laura de Noves, was his private life all that it should have been, at least two illegitimate offspring being charged to his loose amours.

But the death of Laura in 1348 seems to have made a great change in his manner of life, although it did not lessen very much his love of the applause of the great. He had taken part in the Rienzi revolution at Rome in 1347 against his former friends the Colonnas, and the same year had built a house at Parma with the

idea of living there the quiet but honoured life of a
poet, and surrounding himself with a few old and
tried friends. Several of these died, however, about
the same time as Laura, and so all his plans were
changed. He became morose and religious. He gave
up poetry and devoted himself again to humanistic
pursuits. His theory of humanism was that the orator
and the poet should educate themselves so as to present to the world as human beings, perfect and per-
sonified forms of beautiful prose and verse. And in
classing Petrarch as a humanist we must not confuse
that term with the title given to the classical scholars
of the two following centuries, or with the radical
movement of thought which they encouraged under
that name. Petrarch's humanism recognized and in
part inculcated Christianity, that of Pontano and Valla
and the other later so-called humanists, rebelling
against ecclesiastical authority, was destined to weaken
morality and encourage scepticism and indifference to
good and evil. Self culture and self effectuation in
unison with revealed religion were the watchword and
the aim of the Petrarchan cult of humanism, while the
professors of the later and more revolutionary movement, venerating antiquity above everything else, and

strongly tainted with pedantry, were to make light of Christianity and an open parade of paganism.

And while I am dwelling upon the nobility of Petrarch's humanism, I may here refer to other laudable pursuits which it brought in its train. He studied philosophy and ethics, and decked out many precepts of morality with all the graces of pure and ornate language. Such subjects as the " Remedies of Fortune," " True Wisdom," " The Contempt of the World," " Government," " Avarice," " His own Ignorance of Himself and Others," were all beautifully treated by him, and although these writings would not be received seriously in the present age of moral and philosophical discussion, they were no doubt useful and interesting at the time.

He was a great searcher, too, after the works of antiquity, in an age when Italian libraries were sparsely endowed and the works and authenticity of the classic writers often lost or hopelessly confounded. He spent much time in endeavouring to gather together the productions of such authors as Livy, Varro, Quintilian and Cicero, and also in the study of the Greek masters.

The last twenty years of the great scholar and poet's life were otherwise uneventful. He moved to the little

PETRARCH.

hamlet of Arqua for more solitude and reflection in
1369, retained the close friendship and fellow-student-
ship of Boccaccio for the rest of his life, and was
found dead in his library in 1374.

In spite of all I have said of the choiceness and
purity of Petrarch's language, the perfection of his
metre, and that inborn melody by which a musical
resonance comes from the very pronunciation of his
words, there is a certain sameness in all his poetry
which makes it monotonous, and there is, perhaps, too
much generality in his descriptions, both of persons
and inanimate nature. One can detect all through a
similarity of phrase and idea which his mastery of
rhyme and arrangement does not altogether hide.
There is, too, in many of his works a tendency to
ornate rhetoric and stylistic trifles which gives one the
idea that the author is approaching his subject more
as an artist than a thinker, and is aiming more at
perfection of form than of matter.

And there are some traits of character about
Petrarch besides those already mentioned which, in
spite of his great learning and his brilliance as a man
and a poet, one cannot admire. Unlike his friend
Boccaccio he was jealous of the great Dante and, it is

said, refused to read the " Divina Commedia " at all.
Intense egotist and autocrat, too, that he was, he
would brook no rival near that literary throne which
he claimed as his very own, and yet he was always
discontented, preoccupied, wearied with life, and per-
turbed by its trivial disappointments.   Although the
first man of letters of his time, and the possessor in
later life of both honours and riches, he seemed to be
continually given over to melancholy and to incapacity
for satisfaction.

But how many brilliant parts, if they are accompanied by extraordinary contradictions and idiosyn-
crasies, entered into the makeup and character of this
remarkable Italian.   The continual proclaimer of
liberty for his enslaved and downtrodden country, yet
the consortor with and willing tool of her worst
tyrants.   The life-long heralder and exponent of the
rarest female charms and virtues and of ideal womanhood in his adoration of Laura de Noyes, yet, withal
an unbridled libertine.   To-day the recluse and hermit
pursuing the quiet study of nature amid the mountain
fastnesses of Vaucluse, to-morrow the clever, eloquent
and richly-robed ambassador to the sparkling and
pompous courts of kings and popes.   The upholder

of imperial and papal rule at Rome for one moment, the ardent advocate of republicanism the next. The devoted patriot, and at the same time anxious above everything else for his own personal glorification. The great lyrist who first sang in Italy of individual instead of allegorical and mystical love, and yet more humanist than poet, and philosopher, politician, historian, and orator as well. Never in Italian, and rarely in any country's literature, has a star of so many different hues shone forth, nor a genius more varied or versatile, nor a being evolved from so many contradictory elements, been encountered among the race of men.

THE GREAT POETS OF ITALY.

TO PETRARCH.

I.

Bard of Arrezo, Tuscan son,
  Who for Italia justly won
The scholar's wreath of bays.
  Who turned from law's and priestcraft's wiles
To sing of Laura's rapturous smiles,
  And Love's more gentle ways.

II.

On whose devotion to that name
  Rests more secure his right to fame
Than on those other parts
  He played, the princely delegate,
Interpreter of things of state,
  And politician's arts.

III.

A myth 'tis said she may have been,
  This airy thing, this beauty's queen;
Perchance a charming maid.
  Yet others say a matron she,
Blessed with a numerous progeny,
  The spouse of Hugh de Sade.

PETRARCH.

IV.

But whether matron, maid, or myth,
 The verse he decked his Laura with
In madrigal and ode,
 In sonnet and in roundelay,
For Petrarch surely paved the way
 To glory's dazzling road!

V.

One long melodious monody
 To her in fervent loyalty
His ardent soul outpoured.
 No sweeter gems of canzoniere
E'er melted on a human ear,
 No female more adored.

VI.

I see him leave his Pisan home
 When Clement moved from ancient Rome
His throne to fair Provençe.
 The boy along Avignon's streets,
Watching the pontiffs, their retreats
 With battlements ensconce.*

---

* Avignon is still encircled by the ramparts built by the popes of the 14th century. The walls which are of great strength are surmounted by machicolated battlements, flanked at intervals by thirty-nine massive towers. This immense and powerful structure forms one of the finest examples of mediæval fortifications in existence. In those days of temporal as well as spiritual power, popes as well as kings had apparently to guard well their own.

THE GREAT POETS OF ITALY.

VII.

I see his stern, ambitious sire
　　Consign to the relentless fire
Those tomes the lad adored.
　　Yet does the parent kind forego
That Virgil and that Cicero,
　　When tearfully implored.

VIII.

I see him later, near life's noon,
　　With lovely nature close commune
'Mid hills and dales delights,
　　Among her limestone ledges mount
To trace fair Sorgnès to her fount
　　In wild Vaucluse's heights.

IX.

And from that far seclusion, he
　　Could look upon impartially
Those struggles and affrays
　　Which in his time upheaved and tore
His native land, and had before,
　　In Alighieri's days.

PETRARCH.

X.

I see, in modern culture's list,
    His name stand high. Great humanist
Who gave new learning birth.
    To which his gems of lyric art,
And all the sweets his songs impart,
    Appear of minor worth.

XI.

How well Vaucluse, that deathless name,
    In thee revived the dormant flame
Of learning's smouldering fire.
    How sweet Avignon, through thy halls
There pealed those dulcet madrigals,
    The music of that lyre.

XII.

He left to a succeeding age
    To darken humanism's page
With scepticism and doubt.
    To him with faith's consoling light
The torch of learning burned more bright
    With paganism left out.

THE GREAT POETS OF ITALY.

Petrarch! Though discord troublesome
   Exiled thee from thy native home,
Strange cities to behold;
   Yet Rome rejoiced in time to see
A worthier crown bestowed on thee
   Than Scipio's of old.

And old and modern eras met
   When on thy brow the wreath was set
On Jove's eternal hill.
   When the renaiscent morning burst
To quench the human spirit's thirst,
   To lessen human ill.

Standing without the closing door
   Of mediæval mystic lore,
'Twas thine to well survey
   The kingdom of the modern thought.
Thou scholar-bard, who well had wrought
   For learning's brighter day.

PETRARCH.

XVI.

But Nature's haunts could not enchain
   Thee, Petrarch, thou wert ever vain;
Ambition made thee go
   To Parma, where a tyrant bold
Had conquered what he could not hold,*
   Thy friend Correggio.

XVII.

And though when Laura came to die
   A calmer life thou then didst try,
There still within thee ran
   That wish to mingle with the great,
And despots ruled again thy fate,
   The tyrants of Milan.

XVIII.

How many contradictions are
   Apparent in thy character,
Renowned Arrezian.
   To-day a monarchist sincere,
To-morrow sees thee fearless wear
   The garb republican.

---

* While the tyrant Azzo di Correggio freed Parma from the perhaps greater tyranny of the Lords of Verona in 1341, neither he nor his family could hold it long, and it came into the hands of the more powerful Viscontis in 1346.

THE GREAT POETS OF ITALY.

XIX.

One day arrayed in peasant dress,
  Roaming Vaucluse's wilderness,
Content with simple things;
  The next the wandering bard no more,
But the rich-robed ambassador
  Before the courts of kings.

XX.

Yet great thy gifts and genius were,
  Whom tyrant and deliverer
Alike their counsel made.
  Though Florence hid from thee her face,
Thou hast a worthy resting place
  'Neath Arqua's olive shade.

LUDOVICO ARIOSTO.

PART III.

—

ARIOSTO

ARIOSTO

Ludovico Ariosto, born at Reggio, September 8th, 1474.
Died at Ferrara, June 6th, 1533.

THE fame of Ludovico Ariosto, the epic poet of the
Renaissance, and his claim to a high place in Italian
literature rests on one work alone. If he had not left
us that thrilling story in verse of the ravings of
Orlando for the beautiful Angelica, who has married
another, with its many anecdotes and borrowed episodes thrown in—the whole included under the well-
known title, " Orlando Furioso "—he would have no
other claim to a place here or in any collection of the
world's great poets. I would not want it inferred from
this that Ariosto left no other worthy verse. His seven
satires, in some of which he severely castigated his
late master, the parsimonious and ungrateful Ippolito
D'Este, were famous at the time, as well as his con-
tributions to Italian drama in the form of many

comedies, chief among them " Cassaria Suppositi,"
" La Lena," " Il Negromante," and the " Scolastica."
Nearly all these plays were first written in prose and
then transformed into verse. They were composed to
please his later and more generous patron, Alphonso,
who delighted in theatrical performances. Presented
before the leading families of his province, these
comedies brought applause and renown to Ariosto at
the time of their production, but, unlike the " Orlando
Furioso," they did not live in Italian literature and
after their author's time were soon forgotten. They
abound in immoralities but no more so than the general
dramatic productions of that period.

Ludovico Ariosto was born on September 8th, 1474,
(one authority* says at Modena, another at Reggio),
the eldest of the ten children of Nicolo and Daria
Ariosto. His father was the commander of the citadel
of Reggio; his mother belonged to the wealthy and
noble family of Malaguzzi, but if she brought any
wealth to her husband it had apparently all vanished
before the latter's death. Ariosto was another example
of how nearly the profession of law succeeded in
depriving the literature and poetry of Italy of what

* Everett.

was to prove one of their brightest ornaments. Ariosto Senior insisted on the boy, although he had early shown a strong inclination towards poetry and letters, wasting five full years of his life in the pursuit of legal studies, always distasteful to the young Reggian student. His early years were steeped in hardship and misfortune. Deprived of his father by death ere he had reached manhood, there fell upon him, at an age when most ambitious young Lombardians were cultivating the muse and higher education at the universities, the care of his widowed mother and the large family of younger brothers and sisters all left comparatively penniless. For, though the father, Nicolo, belonged to an influential and titled family, he had never taken advantage of his opportunities to provide his own large progeny with a competence and had apparently wasted any portion his wife had brought him. Like his great follower, Tasso, who was not to see the light till eleven years after the subject of this sketch had breathed his last, young Ariosto, too, fell under the spell of the D'Estes of Ferrara and although never imprisoned or forced to wander from place to place for a livelihood, like the author of the " Gerusalemme Liberata," the treatment which the princely family meted out to Ariosto seems to have been niggardly in the extreme and in no wise commensurate with the great work that he accomplished for them or for his times. He first attached himself to the Court of the Cardinal Ippolito, who, attracted by a prose comedy and some light lyrics which Ariosto as a mere youth had composed, seems to have looked upon the gifted young writer more as a messenger and a court jester than an author and paid him a salary little better than that of a menial servant. The Cardinal's knowledge of letters was scanty and his appreciation of the dedication to himself of the "Orlando Furioso" was only shown by some light joking remark and no pecuniary reward. Bitterly sensible of all this ingratitude after his efforts of over eleven years, and dissatisfied with the irregular instalments in which his small allowance was doled out to him, Ariosto fell out with the Cardinal, and rather than yield to the latter's demands to accompany him on an expedition to Hungary in 1518, he resigned from his service. The Cardinal's brother, Alphonso, Duke of Ferrara, had in the meantime made use of the young author's learning and diplomatic gifts by sending him at Ippolito's instigation on two different occasions as ambassador to Pope

ARIOSTO.

Julius II, first, when his Holiness had threatened war against Ferrara, and a second time after the papal forces had been defeated. So successful had the young poet's efforts been that on his making application to the Duke for assistance after his severing his relations with the Cardinal (who in the meantime had died), the former appointed him Governor of Grafagnana, a distant Appenine province attached to the Dukedom of Ferrara and then in a state of revolt and civil war. Here young Ariosto remained three years, winning by his prudence and tact not only the thanks of his patron but also the affection and entire submission to authority of the inhabitants of the former rebellious province. On his return to Ferrara he busied himself with his comedies and satires and thankfully acknowledged the kindness of the Duke, so much more generous and beneficent a patron than the Cardinal did Alphonso prove to be. And yet when it is considered how much he did for Alphonso and how he immortalized him by his muse, one does not wonder that Ariosto afterwards complains that neither of his Ferrarese masters had done all they should for him.

The last years of Ariosto's too short life were tranquil and happy. A beautiful mansion and garden at

THE GREAT POETS OF ITALY.

Ferrara, some say built for him by his patron, others, provided by his own frugality, afforded him a convenient retirement where he could revise his great work of "Orlando Furioso" and undertake and complete other minor works. He also now superintended the erection of a theatre in which his own comedies were among the most important of the plays presented. The "Orlando Furioso" had been revised once since 1515 and reprinted a third time in 1521. Only a year before its author's death it appeared again in a new and remodelled dress. The fourth, or 1532 edition, is the form in which it still appears. It was first printed in forty-six books, but twelve years after Ariosto's death five more books he had written on the same subject were added to it. Relieved from the cares of official life, he had been untroubled as so many of his preceding and succeeding fellow poets had been and were to be by banishment, political and military disturbances or the real or imaginary slights or neglect of their ideal women. Although Ariosto did not attain to old age, his closing days in their calm and serene quiet may be said to be unique for one so important and exalted in the State and at a time so given to strife and warfare of all kinds. He died on the 6th of June,

ARIOSTO.

1533, of consumption. He had been an abnormally fast eater and suffered from indigestion. He might have lived longer had not the physicians resorted to such violent remedies to get rid of the first complaint that they brought their patient to so weakened a condition that his last malady seized on him with rapidly fatal results.

Ludovico Ariosto was a man of great eminence in the social world as well as in that of literature. In the former he moved among and had the affection and esteem of the first in the land. Included among his close intimates, beside the great D'Este family, were the mighty Medici and the best of the Popes. Leo the Tenth, the great papal benefactor of literature and art, honoured Ariosto with his friendship and his patronage but unfortunately died before he had much opportunity to greatly assist in the poet's worldly advancement. In the letters of his country Ariosto lived long enough to see himself assured of permanent fame. Few works have been so often printed as the " Orlando Furioso." It has passed through nearly a hundred editions and been printed not only in every European country but also in all the languages of the world.

Whether Ariosto was ever actually laureated for his

great work has been the subject of much discussion. Some authorities state that he was publicly crowned at Mantua by Charles the Fifth in 1532 but the weight of opinion is against this. His inclinations at this time were towards seclusion. He had only finally completed the work late in 1532 and his fatal illness very speedily followed, so there would be very little time for a public coronation in the short interval.

The best students and biographers of the Italian poets tell us that Ariosto was modest and affable, rather inclined to melancholy, though sprightly in the society of women. He was the enemy of ceremony and servility, abstemious in his diet, only eating one meal a day and often woke and wrote during the night. His disposition was timid. On both land and water he seemed to be always guarding against either real or imaginary perils, but his integrity was admitted by all. He was rather above middle size, had black curly hair, black sparkling eyes, large nose, stooped shoulders and a slow and deliberate walk and action.

While Ariosto undoubtedly had some secret amours, women did not trouble him in the way in which they seem to have continually occupied the time and were the chief source of inspiration of many of the other great Italian poets. But he admired the fair sex greatly, was well versed in the deeds and accomplishments of all the great women of antiquity, and was thus justly entitled to be called the Italian poet of chivalry. If he ever married, it was never publicly announced. He left two sons, Virginia and Baptista, some authorities say by Alexandra, the widow of one Strozzi, whom Ariosto is said to have secretly espoused late in life. Others allege that Ariosto was too fond of liberty to bind himself, either to the orders of the Church or in wedlock, and that the sons were natural, each by a different mother. Be this as it may, both attached themselves to the ducal house of Ferrara and both seem to have attained high distinction in the service of the D'Estes, one in the Church, the other in the Army.

Ariosto had fallen upon the world in the midst of a brilliant age, a period of great men and great events. The Renaissance had dawned. Old feudal dynasties were giving way to new and more liberal ones; new worlds were being discovered; thought was becoming resistless and aggressive; art had reached a period of matchless splendour; a band of learned men had arisen in Italy who were inculcating the study of

THE GREAT POETS OF ITALY.

Plutarch, Aristotle, Plato and the other great Greek
masters; a human individuality wanting in the Middle
Ages had arisen in Italy and men were now being
valued more for their personal merit than for their
birth. Other crowns besides a heavenly one were
beginning to attract the ambitions of mankind, with
the result that indifference to good and evil, in other
words scepticism, was becoming rampant. This revival
of learning, this contempt for mediæval mysticism, this
deviation from the poetry of Dante and Petrarch and
the prose of Boccaccio into the channels of classical
research, was threatening Italy with pedantry and
paganism. The professors of this new cult of " humanism," as it was called, though far different from the
noble and Christian humanism of Petrarch, had
acquired the habits of puerility of style, of vanity of
rhetoric, and of the stupidity of tedious quotation. All
these classic weaknesses combined hung like a dark
and enveloping cloud over the national literature, and
it was only the influence of Florence and the illustrious
and scholarly Lorenzo de Medici that saved Italy from
again being latinized. Though in private life a libertine and given to the grossest immoralities, not only
was Lorenzo great as the public patron of art and let-

ters, but also profound himself in that scholarship which saw the best results in insisting on the assimilation of classical models with modern feeling in Italian literature. Both idealist and realist himself, he drew equally from the classic and the modern schools of thought and encouraged this happy combination among the learned men of his time. But when Ariosto arrived upon the scenes all this intellectual and educational advance and magnificence had been to a large extent retarded in Italy by the din and the hatred of civil war. Her poets and her men of letters had not been able, by reason of this upheaval, to take full advantage of that spirit of enterprise which was inspiring their brethren in foreign lands.

In spite of all the advances in other lines of thought and action, poetry since the time of Petrarch and Boccaccio had not made an equal progress. Instead of attempting the creation of something new, Italian poets had satisfied themselves with being only copiers of the old Romanticists who had gone before. Uberti and Frezzi had produced poor imitations of the "Divina Commedia," Orgagna had brought out some comic works, Pucci and others had transformed history into verse. The drama had received an impetus in Mussato's "Eccerinus." Lorenzo de Medici, great idealist and realist combined as he was, as I have just intimated, had saved Italian literature from entire submersion by "humanism," and had brought lustre upon his family name, as well as upon Tuscany, by uniting in his poetry all the refinements of the classical world of long ago in which he really lived, and had contributed much to both drama and pastoral poetry. But the chivalry from which the old masters had taken their songs of love and war had passed away before Ariosto's day and only the misty legends connected with the adventures of that honoured age remained. Poetry seemed therefore in the midst of all these other material and intellectual advances to have been relegated to the school of imitative romance. Among the only mediocre writers of this intervening period were Pulci, who wrote the heroic poem "Morgante Maggiore" in Florentine patois, and spoilt his epic of the converted giant by burdening it with long and tedious tales of eating and drinking and lists of savoury dishes and by writing in a scoffing and irreligious vein. Berni, who followed, was chiefly noted as the reviser of Boiardo's "Orlando Innamorato." He was the leader of his time in satire and burlesque but was cut off by poison through an intrigue of one of the Medici too early in life to permit of a fair judgment being passed upon his genius. But if he did nothing else, he left a name for that mocking style of poetry which Byron was afterwards so forcefully to adopt.

It was little to be wondered at therefore that by Ariosto's time the reading and the listening public, the lettered world of the day, had sickened of all the weak and hackneyed imitations that were being dished up to them and longed for something original, or at least for some more attractive and enlivening way of presenting the old romances. This they found in Ariosto for although he adhered to the old plan and instead of creating and mapping out a new plot and a new story fell back on Boiardo's "Orlando in Love," the author of which had died before completing, yet the metamorphosis was so complete, the additions and embellishments so unsparing, that the two could scarcely be recognized as being from the same original. While the style of Boiardo was laboured and heavy, that of Ariosto was lively, rapid and direct and nearer to that of the great master of style, Homer, than the productions of any other Italian poets had been. The "Orlando Furioso" may be said to be a law unto itself

and unlike any other poem of its own or any other
time. A strange mixture it surely is of the comic and
the satiric, the light and the licentious, the heroic, the
descriptive, and the tender. Ariosto depicts his hero
as maddened by the loss of his Angelica, who, having
escaped from both Orlando and his rival Rinaldo outside the walls of Paris, rescues and weds a young war-
rior, Medoro, after which, apparently in bold defiance of
Charlemagne and his two kinsmen, her former lovers,
the newly-wedded pair carve their joint names on
every tree and wall and cave surrounding their retreat.
These inscriptions, discovered by the searching and
distracted Orlando, lead to his insanity, only cured
after a long space by the remedy which the paladin
Astolfo finds in his winged flight to the moon, whither
he is guided by St. John the Evangelist. This is only
one of the countless airy and unreal tales which
Ariosto weaves into his long romance of forty-six
books. He pads the story with legends of every country, notable personage and period in which the adventures and episodes of knights and ladies, hermits and
sorcerers, demons and angels are continually portrayed.
He makes no pretence to originality of conception but
borrows and copies openly and without disguise, not

only from contemporaries, but also from the writings of Homer and Virgil and nearly all the other famous poets of antiquity.

And yet in spite of this flagrant plagiarism there is an absence of tedium in the " Orlando Furioso " which keeps the interest of the reader engaged and which is wanting in the works of all the other romanticists who preceded Ariosto. The long and otherwise tiresome recital of the main narrative is repeatedly coloured and enlivened by a sparkling diversion to some well-told story of war or love from the older poets. Humour, too, shines forth throughout the whole work and the verse and measure in which it is composed are unsurpassed. His style is lively and rich in description and imagination. As far as minuteness of detail is concerned he is precise except in depicting natural scenery. Here he could not lay claim, as the English Wordsworth could, to be called an analyser of nature, although the following stanza, translated by Mr. Everett, is hard to surpass as a description of rustic beauty:

"Of fragrant laurel trees were charming bowers
 Of palms and of the loveliest myrtle there,
 Cedars and oranges with fruit and flowers

THE GREAT POETS OF ITALY.

Entwined in varied forms, which all were fair,
Gave with their thick shade from the scorching powers
In summer days delectable repair,
And through the branches moved with careless flight
Pouring their song the minstrels of the night."

The great blot upon Ariosto's peerless work was the
fulsome praise bestowed all through it upon the family
of D'Este and his efforts to trace their descent from
the heroes and even the gods of antiquity. While
Orlando is the nominal hero, Ruggiero the ancestor
of the lords of Ferrara is made the real one, the accom-
plisher of the most wonderful deeds recounted. Of
course this is no worse than the nauseating encomiums
of the great found in the works of other Italian poets
of that age and in those of our own Spenser and
Dryden and the other English poets, who owed all
they had or hoped for to the patronage of those in
high places. But considering the scanty measure of
reward doled out to Ariosto by the lords of Ferrara
and the different occasions where he himself refers to
and bewails this niggardly treatment, it seems at least
inconsistent if not cowardly in him to bestow such
unmerited praise as he does upon his parsimonious and
indifferent patrons.

ARIOSTO.

But in spite of this drawback, with its infinite variety
of theme, its faultless verse and measure, its keenness
of detail, its mastery of style, its humour, its occasional peeps into mythology and the mystic and supernatural, its tales of love and jealousy and demoniacal
fury, its records of suffering and triumph, its episodes
from Homer and Virgil and the other Ancients cleverly altered to suit his own story, the genius of Ariosto
has certainly presented to the world in the " Orlando
Furioso " an artistic structure in words unrivalled in
his own country except by the Ancients themselves,
and in ours surpassed alone by Shakspeare, though
equalled perhaps by Milton. Space far beyond my
limit would be required to convey to the reader an
adequate description of the many beauties of the work,
the deeds of its chivalric knights and charming ladies,
their songs of love and war, their noble steeds, their
stately halls and matchless gardens of flowers, foun-
tains and terraces, their velvet lawns studded with magnificent trees and the vast forests with their beasts of
prey, surrounding the great ancestral demesnes here
pictured. To fully appreciate the " Orlando Furioso "
the English student of poetry requires first to be a
genuine lover of high romance. Next he must pos-

sess himself of one of the best translations obtainable and this will require not only to be hurriedly glanced through but that every part be given the most careful study and analysis.

Ariosto wrote not for posterity but only for his own generation. He was an artist merely for the love of his art. He strove for perfection in form and style; not to hand down to future generations a work containing any great moral lesson or any serious purpose. His subject, "Orlando," was a threadbare one and would never in itself have kept the "Furioso" alive. It was the magical and indescribable manner in which Ariosto's genius endowed his subject that has ensured its immortality. Nowhere else in Italian letters is to be found such a rare combination of poem, romance, epic and drama. In the works of this seeming improvisator, yet really deep scholar, there may be said to be included all the learning and all the faith of the Renaissance. And in him the stanzaic framework which he adopted, the Ottava Rima, reached a higher pinnacle of perfection in grace and beauty than in the hands of any other Italian poet.

ARIOSTO.

TO ARIOSTO.

I.

Long after Dante sang the woes of Dis,
   And of the heavenly joys of Beatrice told,
A cycle after Petrarch dreamed in bliss,
   Of Laura and her virtues manifold;
While on the crest of Ocean's vast abyss,
   The dauntless Genoese tempestuous roll'd,
And Italy yet groaned 'neath lurid war
There dawned at Reggio Ariosto's star.

II.

Ere this, to Florence 't had been given to save
   Italian letters from a shameless dower,
For humanism had threatened to enslave
   All modern thought with its pedantic power,
Of puerile style and pagan speech—a wave
   Her youthful lore had threatened to devour,
When great Lorenzo came and joined the ideal,
The ancient classic thought, with modern real.

III.

Brilliant the time when on the world there shone
   The offspring of Emilia's gifted breed,
Though unkind fate had early made him groan
   Beneath the tyrant yoke of D'Estes need;

107

THE GREAT POETS OF ITALY.

Yet all his fortune with Ferrara thrown,
  How well from these had he his genius freed,
To change with art and style and humour strong,
The weak effect of Boiardo's song.

IV.

Happy it was that Ariosto came,
  To light again the old Dantean fire,
For Frezzi's empty song, servile and lame,
  No longer new resounded but to tire.
Men asked for epic of more lofty aim
  Than Pulci struck from his irreverent lyre,
And something, too, more knightly, less grotesque
Than Berni's wit and mimicking burlesque.

V.

So Ariosto's master mind took hold,
  And from divining stars and sorcery
The rarest tales evolved, sublime and bold;
  The lovers' names entwined on grot and tree,
Alcina to her garden from the wold,
  Ruggiero alluring soothingly;
The kidnapped maiden in the Hebrides,
Rockbound and torn by monsters of the seas.

108

ARIOSTO.

VI.

Thus all this medley of the false and true
  Swift passes in kalediscopic sight
Of lurking beast, of forests varied hue,
  Of mansion fair, of revel blithe and bright.
What stately halls and courtyards in review!
  With lovely lady and with gallant knight,
What riders on their chargers prancing gay!
What maidens singing soft their roundelay!

VII.

A complex framework round which close were wove
  Enchantment, passion, chivalry and hate.
Behold Orlando, how he, maddened, strove
  Medoro and Angelica t'unmate;
See Christian Bradamante's undying love
  To Pagan Ruggiero consecrate,
The consummation of that holy flame
From which the mighty race of Este came.

VIII

And he tells, too, in faultless stirring verse
  Of poor Orlando all with madness hewn,
Raving beneath his frenzy's blighting curse,
  Till paladin Astolfo in the moon,

THE GREAT POETS OF ITALY.

While coursing through the astral universe,
  Discovers reason's full restoring boon,
The bottled minds of men, besides his own
He also finds and brings Orlando's down.

IX.

" For," says the song, " in Luna is a spot
  Where gather all the things of earth mislaid,
The glory of great empires long forgot,
  The tears and sighs of loving ones betrayed;
And close-sealed phials in a countless lot
  Where wandering minds of men are oft conveyed,"
So, saturate with that essence from above,
Orlando's cured of madness and of love.

X.

Heedless of space and unconfined by time,
  The bard embraces every zone and shore,
From Afric's deserts and her tropic clime
  To northern lands with mere and river frore:
He paints the storm, he sings of stress and crime,
  Of struggling ships, of billows' surge and roar
From orient ports, where pope and priest hold sway
To pagan Indus and to far Cathay.

ARIOSTO.

XI.

How happy that it was not asked of thee,
   Great Reggian bard, that from thy native land
Thou should'st an outlaw and expatriate be,
   To wander exiled on a foreign strand;
Nor forced o'er distant mountain slopes to flee,
   Seared with the unrequited lover's brand,
These were the fates of other poets; thine,
To pen thy verse contented and benign.

XII.

And, thou who on laborious stanzas wove
   The shafts of fury, lighted the dull page
With bursts of chivalry and gleams of love,
   While history opened on a brighter age;
How well with thee romance and epic throve,
   To whom was given that envied heritage,
To weave rich fiction, marvels rare unfold,
Which rival Homer's matchless songs of old.

MICHAEL ANGELO.

PART IV.

MICHAEL ANGELO

MICHAEL ANGELO

Michael Angelo Buonarroti, born at Caprese, March 6th, 1474. Died at Rome, February 18th, 1564.*

I MAY be open to censure for including this remarkable man—far more remarkable in the other fine arts than in the realm of poetry—among the seven most notable Italian poets. There are so many others of whom it may be truly said that devotion to the muse was so much more largely their chief calling in life than his, and no doubt the important events of his life may be more appropriately and fully told in a work dealing with great painters and sculptors rather than with poets and poetry.

I admit there is, on the face of it, some reason for taking this position. Michael Angelo Buonarroti's fame is undoubtedly greater in the realms of painting and sculpture than in that of poetry. But it cannot be

---

* Everett says 1563.

deduced from this alone that he was not one of the greatest of Italian poets, and my justification for including him here is that no one can properly argue that the mere fact of his having attained to the very highest pinnacle of fame as a painter and a sculptor can detract from the exalted and eminent place he took in his third and late choice in life, Italian verse. Moreover, the very exceptional circumstances surrounding the poetry he wrote—his advanced age, the mighty name he had already made for himself in the other fields just mentioned, his platonic affection for young Cavalieri, his reverence for and loyalty to the widow of Pescara, his worship of ideal beauty, not beauty in its personal and specific manifestations but in the universal and the impersonal—all these, apart altogether from the strict literary merit of his verse, must surely entitle Michael Angelo to a high and worthy place among the bards of his native country.

He was one of the great Florentines, though not actually born there, the family being away at Caprese where the father, Ludovico Buonarroti, was temporary governor under the Medici, at the date of Michael Angelo's birth on the 6th of March, 1474. The family

MICHAEL ANGELO.

boasted of noble descent* but Ludovico was never capable of earning more than a bare living for his family, and was too proud to engage in trade. Michael Angelo's mother was delicate from his birth and died a few years afterwards, and it is recorded that he had to be nursed when an infant by a foster-mother, the wife of a neighbouring marble-worker. Early in life the boy showed a strong predisposition towards art, especially sculpture, having as he said, " sucked in the passion with his foster-mother's milk." His father, being ambitious though poor, had higher aims than this for his son, but after many solicitations agreed to the lad following his chosen calling, and at thirteen he began the career of a painter with the famous Brothers Ghirlandaio.

To follow the young artist through his many trials and triumphs, both in painting and sculpture, and later on in architecture, until while still a comparatively young man he became far and away the leader of the then known world in all these arts, would be presumption on my part. Many others more profound in scholarship and better informed on the subjects themselves

---

* Florence Trail says (p. 111) that Michael Angelo's parents were plain people but there is contrary authority to say that the family boasted of noble blood.

117

have accomplished this task so much more fully and ably than I could do, and besides I must not tire my readers by such a digression, but must remember that I am dealing here with the poet and not with the achievements of men however masterful in the other fields of fine Art. But I may be permitted to say in passing that, soon transferring his attentions to sculpture, while not neglecting painting, under his illustrious patrons, the Medici and afterwards at Bologna and at Rome under Galli Piccolomini Soderini, the Popes Julius II, Leo X and Clement VII, the talented Italian had, by the year 1522, drawn the attention and admiration of the world to himself and his own City of Florence by his numerous, rare and unchallenged works, many of them preserved to this day as the greatest and most priceless treasures of art the world contains. Let me mention only a few, in chronological order. Firstly in sculpture: "Mary lamenting over the Body of Christ," "David," "Cupid," the monument to Julius II, the monuments of the Medici in the Mortuary Chapel of San Lorenzo, "Victory," "The Madonna," "Kneeling Angel," "St. John in the Wilderness," "Virgin and Child," "Madonna and Child," "St. Matthew," "Moses," "Crouching Boy," "Brutus."

MICHAEL ANGELO.

His masterpiece in painting in which he was the contemporary and rival of the great Raphael, is of course the ceiling of the Sistine Chapel at St. Peter's, Rome, which took him nearly five years to accomplish and which involved an enormous amount of physical endurance, most of the work having to be done in a recumbent position, face upwards, to say nothing of the annoyances occasioned by delays in payment and the intrigues of enemies and rivals while the great task was in progress. The toils and difficulties encountered in this vast emprise called from the mighty labourer these almost despairing lines:

" I've grown a goitre by dwelling in this den,
　As cats from stagnant streams in Lombardy
　Or in what other land they hap to be,
　Which drives the belly close beneath the chin.
　My beard turns up to heaven, my nape falls in,
　Fixed on my spine, my breast bone visibly
　Grows like a harp, a rich embroidery
　Bedews my face from brush-drops thick and thin,
　My loins into my paunch like levers grind,
　My buttock like a crupper bears my weight,
　My feet, unguided, wander to and fro,
　In front my skin grows loose, and long behind,
　By bending it becomes more taut and straight.

119

THE GREAT POETS OF ITALY.

Crosswise I strain me like a Syrian bow,
Whence false and quaint I know
Must be the fruit of squinting brain and eye,
For ill can aim the gun that bends awry.
Come then, Giovanni, try
To succour my dead pictures and my fame
Since foul I fare and painting is my shame."

which went to show that although fate had destined
that this was to be the work which far more than anything else was to mark him for immortality it had
become by this time loathsome to its undertaker whose
heart yearned for his marble and his chisel rather than
for his brush. His great painting of " The Last
Judgment " is also in the Sistine Chapel. This he
finished for Pope Clement in 1541. " The Holy
Family," " The Virgin and Child with Four Angels "
and " The Entombment of Christ " (the last two in
the National Gallery at London) are a few others
of the priceless masterpieces of Michael Angelo's
brush which have been handed down to the present
generation.

But now to get at what this article is really intended
for, a sketch of Michael Angelo, the poet. In this
capacity he is unique, not only in his own country, but

MICHAEL ANGELO.

also in any other. England, it is true, can boast of her Blake and her Rossetti, masters in both painting and poetry, and similar boasts may be made by other nations, but in no other land or age in the world's history has there appeared a character of such diverse gifts and all developed to such perfection and fullness of accomplishment as Michael Angelo. He has been well named the greatest soul of his century and the sublimest genius of the world and an English writer* has said that the thought of another Michael Angelo in any land is impossible.† He had written some love ditties in the early days at Bologna but it was not till after all the great achievements I have already

---

* Sir James Stephen.

† In their luminous and discursive work entitled "A History of the Italian States," Messrs. Stafford and Ball on page 29 of the introduction in Vol. I venture the assertion that Leonardo Da Vinci the great painter and sculptor (1452-1519) was also a poet. I have failed after considerable research to confirm this or to find a trace of his writings in verse if he left any such. His gifts were indeed various, perhaps more so than those of Michael Angelo, for they embraced in a high degree architecture, music, engineering and natural philosophy besides sculpture and painting. He was a master of both art and science. But in spite of Messrs. Stafford and Ball's claim to the contrary poetry does not seem to have been one of Leonardo Da Vinci's attainments. In their article on Italian Literature the compilers of the Encyclopædia Britannica it is true go so far as to state that he was a poet but in their somewhat exhaustive biographical sketch of this great Italian (Vol. 16, p. 444) no reference is made to any of his poetical works. We may therefore conclude that if these existed they were trifling and unimportant.

121

recorded and after he had attained his sixtieth year
that the long pent elements of fervour and tenderness
in the great artist's nature found utterance in verse.
And then there was no idea of publicity or of pecuniary gain. The sonnets and other poems were merely
sent to friends, some of whom they were dedicated to,
and all remained in manuscript for over half a century after their author's death. And even then they
were given to the world far differently to the originals
as left by the great sculptor-poet. His grand nephew,
Michael Angelo the Younger, undertook to publish his
uncle's verse but fearing to offend the Church by some
references made to it, being over-nice in judging the
grammar and versification of his great relative, and
fearful of the misconstruction of the poems addressed
to young Cavalieri, the young publisher undertook to
alter, add to and subtract from the originals, mere
rough-hewn blockings-out of poems, rather than
finished works of art as they seemed to him, so that
when they did appear they bore no resemblance at all
to what their illustrious author had written. It could not
be expected of Michael Angelo that the poetry which
he was leaving to posterity, could, considering the late
period at which he wrote, the mighty accomplishments

MICHAEL ANGELO.

in sculpture and painting he had wrought and the admittedly narrow range of his poetic mind, be voluminous or bulky. The hand and brain of the most gifted man who ever lived is only capable of a certain amount of effort. Michael Angelo had almost exhausted his mighty energies, both mental and physical, on the rocks of Carrara and—what to any ordinary artist would have seemed an unsurmountable task—the transmutation of the dome of the vast Sistine (flat on his back all the while), from plain plaster to a veritable fairyland of deities, angels, patriarchs and prophets set in the various actions in which they are depicted as being engaged, in a background the most beautiful that imaginative nature can suggest. So that if he has succeeded in adding anything of merit to the poetry of his country under these conditions he is surely entitled to a much higher place in our estimation than if his whole life had been devoted to the muse. His poetry is of the clear-cut, impressive kind. Strange to say he stuck to the Petrarchan model in his verse, not caring, as in the sensuous arts, to strive to establish any precedents in his style. He wrote laboriously and with care to avoid errors—it was the sculptor modelling the beautiful again but this time out of the material of language instead of out of that of marble or of tints and colours. His temperament was all the time restless and suspicious. Twice during his employment by Pietro de Medici and Pope Julius II, imagining himself wronged or in danger, he had taken sudden leave and could with difficulty be persuaded to return to his work. Jealousy also claimed him as her victim and moodily he had refused intimacy with the gentle Raphael, fearful no doubt lest some of his own laurels might be purloined or questioned by his equally illustrious contemporary on canvas.

Elsewhere I have explained that the chief subject matter of the poems of Michael Angelo's age and country was love—a passionate adoration in verse of some marked favourite of the opposite sex. Such had been the theme of his mighty master Dante, and of the great Petrarch who followed him, in their worships, spiritual as it may have been, but essentially personal, of Beatrice and Laura. Such also was to be the magnet which was to attract the immortal bard of Ferrara, who was immediately to follow him whose exploits I am now recording, in that more material and sensual and alas, fatal devotion which he showed to the D'Este sisters. Not so with Michael Angelo. His theme also

MICHAEL ANGELO.

was, indeed, love but it was on a loftier, more ideal plane than any of these. He had drunk deep of the philosophy of Plato and at the same time had come under the wave of the religious revival that had followed the romantic period in Italy and was then being proclaimed by Savonorola in Florence. While he held in contempt the treatment meted out by the factions who controlled the Government of Florence to Dante and Petrarch and other illustrious men of Tuscany he still held his own city in deep affection and always turned to her when other places failed or disappointed him. So that if we discern in the limited verse of Michael Angelo that has been handed down to the present day, instead of devotion of the amorous or the sensual kind, a threefold love of Christ, of Florence, and of Beauty we have not far to go for the reasons for these lofty expressions of his attachment to the ideal and the impersonal rather than to the specific and the individual. His passionate adoration of young Cavalieri and later on of Vittoria Colonna, to both of whom he dedicated much of his verse, would seem at first to contradict this, but a closer study of the works which relate to these two will shew that they were simply his ideals of perfect man and woman, whose loveliness Michael Angelo regarded as merely symbolical of eternal and immutable beauty. I quote here the sonnet dedicated to his ideal lady, as translated by Mr. Symonds. It is typical of most of his poetry and showed the mind of the sculptor and the painter but with a new material—language.

" When that which is divine in us doth try
To shape a face, both brain and hand unite
To give from a mere model, frail and slight,
Life to the stone by Art's free energy,
Thus too before the painter dares to ply
Paint-brush on canvas, he is wont to write
Sketches on scraps of paper and invite
Wise minds to judge his figured history,
So, born a model rude and mean to be
Of my poor self I gain a nobler birth,
Lady from you, you fountain of all worth,
Each overplus and each deficiency
You will make good. What penance then is due
For my fierce heat chastened and taught by you?"

This lady, Michael Angelo declares, had recreated him and inspired in his life a sense of higher things never experienced by him before.

He left behind him no long work in poetry as his master, Dante, had done, for the reasons I have

126

MICHAEL ANGELO.

already explained. His chosen forms of poetic expression were the sonnet and the madrigal. His verse and rhyme show a variety of combination and his thoughts are essentially original. If there is apparent in his word efforts too much absorption in his own skill and a certain amount of obscurity and " aloofness " these must be attributed to the habits of impetuosity and concentration acquired when pursuing the arduous duties of his earlier life. Besides his verse dedicated to Colonna the sonnets to the Supreme Being and to Dante are exquisite for their tenderness and purity.

Michael Angelo, who never married, lived for long after his work as a poet was done. Even his last years were energetic, mostly employed in the architecture of St. Peter's and many of the other great buildings of the Eternal City, where he died in 1564, busy and active to the day of his death. Though moody, taciturn and fitful, in late as in early life, his unchallenged fame and the respect due to his great age, made him, even up to the very time of his final calling away, the most honoured and illustrious citizen of Rome.

If one must be limited to the lives of those great Italians who followed and wrote poetry only in the strict sense and as one of the fine arts, I will no doubt, as I said at the outset, be censured for including in these memoirs Michael Angelo, whose poetry, properly speaking, covered only a narrow and a limited range. But in its broader, nobler and more universal sense, namely, in the creation of the imaginative and the beautiful, can we not get away for a moment from the strict letter of our text to its spirit, and regard the great master artist of Florence as all his life such a creator? Though to us the conceptions of that mighty soul may be intellectually inexhaustible and indefinable, may we not contemplate his whole life's work as one great and sublime poem? Poetry, we must not forget, is something more than mere word painting; it soars in its true comprehension far above the poor human rules of rhyme and measure to the intangible and the inexpressible! The lover of Nature, gazing from some eminence over a vista of green, interspersed with stream and bridge and hamlet and garden stretching below and on to the illimitable blue spreading with its white-capped waves in contrast beyond, sees poetry—deep, universal and beautiful—lying before him. How happy he, if, in addition to this faculty of perception, he has the genius to express the feeling he experiences in language as inspiring as the scene itself?

MICHAEL ANGELO.

How triflingly he regards in comparison to this divine gift the material things of Earth. How little he cares for the sneers and scoffs of the worldly canaille about him,

"The fools unmeaning laugh, the critics hate."

And as another great master of the Art, England's true "bard of beauty," young, poor and inexperienced in worldly things as he was, unknown and unappreciated by the busy, vulgar rabble, and destined alas, so soon to be called hence, saw in the carving on that old weatherbeaten urn in the garden of Holland House those rare mind creations which he was permitted to hand down to us in the word-moulding of his matchless ode, so doubtless this peerless, trebly-gifted Italian before him, gazing on the completed works in marble and fresco, of which he himself was the author, could discern issuing from the product of his hand and brain that same magic voice which said to Keats three centuries afterwards:

"Beauty is Truth, Truth Beauty—that is all
Ye know on Earth and all ye need to know."

THE GREAT POETS OF ITALY.

TO MICHAEL ANGELO.

I.

Thou peerless sculptor, painter bold
  Who shaped Carrara's stone,
Who outlined true the saints of old
  And formed the Holy One,
Whose fresco tells the dire dismay
Of sinners on that dreadful day
  When on the judgment seat
Th' Omnipotent shall sternly sit,
Decrees pronouncing final, fit,
  How marvellous yet meet
That thou in thy maturer age
Shouldst too adorn the muse's page.

II.

What gorgeous tombs of pope and king
  Rose from thy master hand.
What love gods with bewitching wing
  What Davids, virile, grand;
Stern Moses handing down the law
As angered, he base Israel saw
  Before the calf of gold;
The Sweet Madonna, gentle, mild,
Soft smiling on her Holy Child;
  All from the marble cold
Thou didst evolve, and with what grace;
In each a comely form and face.

MICHAEL ANGELO.

III.

Close 'gainst the Sistine's ceiling vault
 Supine for years reclined
Thy wearied frame and without fault
 Thy rare constructive mind
The world's creation fashioned there,
Man driven from his Eden fair,
 The flood, the Sacrifice
Of grateful Noah, huge Goliath
As stricken by the stone, he dieth.
 So boundless thy emprise
That even Haman's fate condign
Is pictured in the vast design.

IV.

And as in marble well thou wrought,
 As thy deft brush in hand
Rich treasure to the canvas brought
 A true magician's wand;
So did thy varied mind inspire
To beauty's love the poet's lyre
 In sonnet and in song;
So in Colonna's praise I see
A spiritual symmetry,
 Carved from the female throng.
A word portrayal to express
A universal loveliness.

131

THE GREAT POETS OF ITALY.

V.

Naught of the rude or commonplace
  In thy love odes I find.
In all thy poetry I trace
  The chaste and cultured mind.
The loftiness of thy designs
With love of beauty intertwines
  The Sculptor's masterpiece
Renewed again in verbal moulds,
Rare vistas to the soul unfolds,
  Outspreading without cease
Bright constellations; from which fall
Beauties serene, impersonal.

VI.

Creator of the fair and bright
  In all their winning ways,
Chisel and brush and pen unite
  With thee in Beauty's praise.
I scan thee, and I learn to look
Beyond the pages of the book
  To the untouched, untold.
For not alone thy polished line,
But all the graces that were thine
  Heaven's harmonies unfold.
And men, alas! can never know
Another Michael Angelo.

TORQUATO TASSO.

PART V.

———

TASSO

TASSO

*Torquato Tasso, born at Sorrento, March 11th, 1544.
Died at Saint Onifrio, Rome, April 25th, 1594.**

THE life of Torquato Tasso, the Italian contemporary of our own Edmund Spenser and the heroic poet of the Italian revival's afterglow, is not hard to write. In fact so full is it of incident, of wandering, of hardship, of the excitement and passion of love and of the general ups and downs of a character naturally restless and unsatisfied yet withal possessing a mind pre-eminently gifted, that the biographer limited to a short space in giving the chief events in this remarkable man's life finds that space exhausted before he feels that he has been at all able to do justice to his subject. Neither are the literary records of Tasso nor those branches of poetry in which he excelled difficult to gather together or explain. Though he was no doubt

---

*Some records say 1595.

a voluminous and exhaustive writer he never attracted a large amount of attention to any of his other works than " Rinaldo," the effort of his youth, his drama of " Aminta," which gave him great local fame, and his last and by far his greatest accomplishment of " Jerusalem Delivered." He died comparatively young, and was not allowed that long period of time in which to spread his efforts over the many fields of literature and song, that other poets of his own and former times attempted to enter upon and excel in. The sorrows of his childhood, the unrequited love of his youth, the wanderings and imprisonment of his later life, the purloining of his best poetic efforts and his sad end all go to make Torquato Tasso the most pathetic figure in Italian literary annals.

The father of Torquato, Bernardo by name, was himself a man of letters and a poet, and the family was an old and influential one which had resided at Bergamo for generations. Bernardo entered the service of the Prince of Salerno as his secretary in 1531 and married the mother of the poet, a beautiful lady of Naples, surnamed Rossi, in 1539. In 1540 he retired temporarily to Sorrento in order to pursue his favourite pastime of poetry, and in this charming spot,

TASSO.

one of the loveliest in the whole world, his illustrious son and second child was born on the 11th of March, 1544. But the fortunes of the father were not destined to last long. Three years after the birth of Torquato, the Prince of Salerno, in dread of assassination at the hands of powerful enemies at Naples, quitted Italy for France, and Tasso senior, loyal to his prince, followed him into banishment leaving young Torquato, then seven years old, with his mother and elder sister at Naples. The family patrimony was confiscated and sentence of death passed on the prince and all his adherents.

The youth was educated by the Jesuit fathers and at ten years of age had acquired a good knowledge of Greek and Latin. He had also learned by this time both poetry and rhetoric and had laid the foundation for that deep religious spirit which permeated his whole after life and gave a sacred title to the great poem which was to make him famous.

His father was permitted to return to Italy again in 1554, and at this time met the Cardinal D'Este, whose name and family were afterwards to be so inseparably associated with the fortunes of his son. With the backing of this powerful family, Bernardo Tasso

137

no doubt felt secure and young Torquato now joined his father at Rome, owing to the retirement of his mother and sister into a monastery through the deprivation of the former's private fortune by her unprincipled brothers. Her death two years afterwards was also laid to their charge.

Torquato was now sent by his father to an influential lady relative at Bergamo on account largely of troubles which were brewing for the elder Tasso at Rome. Here he met the Duke of Urbino and became the companion, in study and in the use of the sword, of the latter's son. After two years spent here in acquiring those accomplishments necessary to the education of a finished Italian gentleman Torquato joined his father at Venice in 1559 and stayed there a year studying Dante and Petrarch, whom, as well as Ariosto, he took for his models, and at sixteen years of age entered the University of Padua, where his father intended he should pursue the study of law. Secretly, however, young Tasso was following up the pursuit of poetry and at eighteen, to the amazement of his friends, he produced the beautiful poem, " Rinaldo," which he had conceived and completed in the short space of ten months. Although his father was grieved at the young man's evident determination to make letters instead of law the ruling occupation of his life, it is said that so soon as he saw and read " Rinaldo " he was so favourably impressed that he reluctantly gave his consent to the change in his son's career.

Although " Rinaldo " did not bring to the youth of eighteen the fame which his " Aminta " or his " Jerusalem Delivered " afterwards brought, it was looked upon by the learned of that day as a marvel for one so young and was received with great acclaim. It was inscribed to the Cardinal Luigi D'Este, into whose employ the young poet's father had now entered. The poem was written in ottava rima, and in it he alludes to the joy he experiences in being relieved from the dry, and to him barren, pursuit of his legal studies in these words:

> " Yet O if Heaven should e'er my wishes crown
> With ease released from law's discordant maze
> To spend on the green turf, in forests brown
> With bland Apollo whole harmonious days,
> Then might I spread Luigi thy renown
> Where'er the sun darts forth resplendent rays."

The year he abandoned law he entered the University of Bologna and devoted himself to the study of the muses and philosophy. He had already conceived the idea of crystallizing into verse the story of Jerusalem and the crusaders, and while at Bologna drafted the first three cantos of the great work. How long he might have stayed here is not known for he now unexpectedly received word that he had been called to the household of the Cardinal D'Este at Ferrara and left the University to join his father at the place which was to be so full of destiny for him, was to see him in turn exalted to high places and cast down to the lowest depths of neglect, imprisonment, unrequited love and despair.

The circumstances surrounding Tasso's arrival at Ferrara were brilliant and promising. One of his patron's family had contracted a matrimonial alliance with a daughter of the Austrian Imperial House and the young poet came on the scene just in time to partake of and be dazzled by all the gay pageantry and splendour attending the royal nuptials. The death of the reigning Pope almost immediately afterward called Luigi to Rome and Tasso was left to amuse and employ himself as he best liked. Thus opened to him the opportunity to meet and cultivate the acquaintance of the two beautiful sisters of the absent Cardinal, the Princesses Lucretia and Leonora. Although they were both much older than the poet, they were highly cultured and fond of poetry, and this soon made the admiration of the sisters and the young author of "Rinaldo" mutual. It also brought about an introduction to another brother, the Duke Alphonso, to whom Tasso decided to dedicate his new and great work of "Jerusalem Delivered," which he was now engaged in writing. On the Cardinal's return further favours awaited young Tasso, no doubt through the influence of the two royal ladies, on whom by now his attractive personality and occasional minor and laudatory poems addressed to them had created a deep and lasting impression. He was permitted to sit with the highest courtiers and with the Duke himself and to meet the men most distinguished both in letters and scholarship and those in exalted positions in the State. He also now met another Lucretia, a famous beauty and a singer of renown who afterwards married into the family of Macchiavelli. To her, too, he addressed many odes and madrigals. It has been suggested that Tasso fell in love with this charming woman, then known as Madame Bendidio, but it would appear rather that he sought more to outrival in literary effort other poets who were also making their addresses to

her than that he was actuated by any amorous motives
of his own.

Bernardo Tasso died in 1569, having lived long
enough to see his promising son on the sure road to
fame. In the following year the Princess Lucretia
married the Count D'Urbino and this threw the
younger sister and the poet more than ever together,
for Leonora D'Este, satiated with worldly pleasure
and deprived of her elder sister's society, now decided
to pursue more congenial tastes in private study and
in the intimacy and companionship of learned and
lettered men. The barriers of conventionality which
had separated them were also beginning to fall through
lengthened intimacy and very frequent commingling
of their fellow-feeling for the attractions of the muse.
It cannot be a surprise, therefore, to find that the
charms of this fascinating and royal lady were now,
with all these opportunities, making deep inroads on
the poet's heart, nor that verses were springing from
his pen breathing towards her soft and bashful senti-
ments like these :

> "Love binds my soul in chains of bliss
> Firm, rigorous, strict and strong,
> I am not sorrowful for this
> But why I quarrel with him is
> He quite ties up my tongue."

TASSO.

In 1570 the poet visited the Court of France with Cardinal D'Este and was made much of by the French king, Charles the Ninth, whose name was soon afterwards to be held in abhorrence owing to its association with the dreadful massacre of St. Bartholomew. Here, too, he met and became a fast friend of the great French poet Ronsard. But the visit to France was not an unmixed success. Either through the intrigues of jealous rivals or for some other cause, some say through his too openly expressed disapproval of the St. Bartholomew massacre, he here lost favour with his patron and under the excuse or privilege of a leave of absence, retired to Rome. But this did not mean a cutting off of all communication with the D'Este family. Rather quite the reverse. The infatuation for the Princess Leonora had gone too far for this and after penning one of his sweetest love songs to her at Tivoli, where she had come to visit her uncle, the great Ippolito, at his beautiful villa and gardens, a journey of only an hour or so from where the poet was himself staying, we find Tasso again, through the influence of the two royal sisters, seeking and obtaining employment in the same influential family, this time with the Duke Alphonso. His circumstances were in reality wonderfully improved by the change. His income was larger and his duties less exacting. He had plenty of time now to follow his poetic inclinations. Not only did he bring to perfection his "Jerusalem Delivered," both in interest of episode and majesty of diction, but he also took advantage of the time he was given by the absence of the Duke in Rome to begin and complete in two months' time his beautiful pastoral dramatic fable of "Aminta," which, in his own country at least, brought him a fame hardly second to the "Jerusalem Delivered."

Tasso's full renown may be said to have been at its zenith when, in the spring of 1573, his "Aminta" was presented before the Cardinal and the Duke and a delighted and distinguished Ferrara assemblage. In this beautiful work, simple in plot and style and with neither fanciful art nor fire, did Torquato Tasso, the man of cultivated mind, of lively fancy and of sensitive temper, pour out from his heart a sweet and limpid strain of pastoral poetry which many Italian singers after him have sought to imitate but none have ever equalled.

He was invited to Pesaro, the residence of the Princess Lucretia, in order that the "Aminta" might be

TASSO.

personally recited before her, and on his return to Ferrara, applying himself diligently to the completion of the " Jerusalem Delivered," he had the satisfaction of seeing the draft of what may be considered his great life effort completed in 1575, in the form of an epic poem of twenty cantos and in eight-lined measure.

But unfortunately, instead of unalloyed and continued good fortune attending this happy consummation, his real troubles were only now beginning. In every walk of man's existence the successful usually incur the envy and suffer the petty slanders of those they have surpassed in life's race. And so it was with Tasso. Jealous intriguers and courtiers, feeling their own inferiority in comparison with his success and popularity, after his " Aminta," began to plot against and undermine the poet with his patron, fearful lest the brilliancy which the " Jerusalem Delivered " would attract to its author should entirely extinguish their own prospects. Guarini and Pigna, his contemporaries, were especially stirred to their most venomous depths. Tasso, in the face of these attempts, resolved to publish his great work dedicated to the Duke, and then to retire to Rome, where he could look for another patron, perhaps equally illustrious and more friendly

to literary effort. In the meantime he had submitted his
work to different friends in Rome for criticism, and
had he listened to and been guided by all or most of
these the result would have been a complete emascula-
tion of the " Jerusalem Delivered." All equally assailed
it and each from a different standpoint. One charged
it with profanity, another that it was derogatory to the
grandeur of the crusade, a third that it questioned the
sanctity of the Church. Others, again, set up metaphysical objections. One critic wished to expugn the
episode of Sophronia and Olindo and set up the charge
of over-embellishment and ornamentality. The most
casual reader of the poem could not fail to recognize
in the personages of Sophronia and Olindo many striking resemblances to the Princess Leonora and the poet
himself, and if Tasso really meant these two characters
to personify his favourite and himself, which is not
doubted, he must have deeply resented the request for
their exclusion.

While he met all these objections with the best of
arguments, yet to satisfy his critics he yielded on many
points and finally the first revision of the " Jerusalem
Delivered " was completed by the end of 1575. But its
author felt keenly that many of its best parts had gone

and disappointment in the delay of publication also seemed to worry him much. He told the Princess Lucretia of his intention to go to Rome and at first she and also the Duke did their best to dissuade him, the latter from fear that he might lose the dedication, which he had now come to look upon as a high honour. However, finally convinced that he was only delaying the publication by urging Tasso to remain, Alphonso at length consented. The poet was well received in Rome, the Cardinal De Medici in particular bestowing on him much attention. But nothing seemed to come of the visit, the poem was not yet published, and we find Tasso very soon back again at Ferrara and received cordially by the Duke in spite of the attentions the poet had received while away from the latter's enemy, De Medici, who even went as far as to make advances for Tasso's transfer to his own Court. But if he had been annoyed by the first revision of the " Jerusalem Delivered," how bitter must have been his feelings when Antoniano and Sperone reviewed it for a second time. The former, as inquisitor as well as critic, demanded the exclusion of all those parts relating to enchantment and love, under pain of preventing any profit from the work, and charged the author with impiety in mingling worldly with holy things in his poem. Sperone claimed that the fable was lacking in unity, a charge which Tasso felt to be more unjust than all the rest. Feeling, however, that these two critics were powerful enough to ruin his prospects if he antagonized them, and since they insisted in their views, Tasso consented with a heavy heart to the further mutilation of his " Jerusalem Delivered," and tells in his after correspondence of the many beautiful things he was forced to exclude, though he did manage to keep for a few intimate friends the original poem in its entirety.

It is hardly necessary here to mention other female attractions which Tasso about this time encountered in the person of Eleonora, the beautiful bride of the Count of Scandiano, and her equally attractive though of course more elderly mother-in-law, the Countess of Sala, both of whom had come to Ferrara to participate in the town's carnival festivities. It has been asserted that the poet fell in love with the younger of the two beauties and some amorous madrigals he dedicated to her have been quoted in proof of this assertion. The better interpretation of these, however, is that they were only written to momentarily withdraw attention

TASSO.

from his more real devotion to Leonora D'Este. So also was the madrigal written to Tarquinia Molza, a famous beauty of Modena, about the same time. But he had further troubles now to contend with which for a time diverted his mind from even the most fascinating of female enchantments. He heard that his " Jerusalem Delivered " was being surreptitiously published throughout the country with no profit to himself and doubtless with errors of both arrangement and printing which would reflect on the author. Alphonso in vain did his best to stop this piracy and the discovery of the fraud had an evil effect on poor Tasso. He had just recovered from the excitement and annoyance of an altercation he had had in the palace of Ferrara with a prying enemy who had opened a chest containing his private papers and with whom he had exchanged blows.* The news of the stealing and printing of his " Jerusalem Delivered " preyed deeply upon his mind, he imagined all kinds of ills were impending, even that his enemies intended to poison

---

* The story has been told by Mr. Wilde, an American writer, how this chest contained papers that revealed the mutual love of Tasso and Leonora, that it was brought to the knowledge of Alphonso who persuaded Tasso to pretend that he was mad and that the latter yielded, thinking to aid his unhappy suit by so doing.

149

him and that he had lost favour with the Church by heresy. He attempted to stab a servant of the Princess Lucretia in her apartments in June, 1577, and the Duke, fearing something more serious might happen, ordered Tasso's temporary confinement, though doing his best to help him and cure him of his strange illusions. At length his conduct became so strange and his complaints and petitions so numerous and annoying, that he was forbidden to communicate with either the Duke or the princesses. This only made him worse and imagining himself abandoned by his best friends and benefactors he resolved on flight. He secretly left Ferrara in June and selecting secluded and unvisited localities for his wanderings and halting places, begged his way along without money or change of raiment until he reached Sorrento where his sister, whom he had not seen since childhood, resided. Fearful of his reception he disguised himself as a messenger from her brother to tell of the latter's illness and want, but finding her deeply grieved threw off his disguise and was welcomed by a display of deep sisterly affection. But no sooner had Tasso been welcomed by his sister and benefitted in health by the variety and beauty of his surroundings at Sorrento than a strange longing overcame him to be back again at Ferrara. The Duke, after much intercession, agreed to receive the prodigal again, but under such harsh terms and a refusal to give the poet his manuscripts and writings, that Tasso this time only stayed there a short time.

We next find him wandering in turn to Mantua, Padua and Venice, then to the Court of Urbino. Dissatisfied even here, though kindly received, he passed on to Piedmont and Turin but his restlessness of mind seemed to prevent him from settling down at any of these places in spite of the many offers of assistance proffered. A longing to again see his old friends at Ferrara and the hope of even yet being able to recover the fruits of his literary labours seem to have impelled him to approach the D'Estes for a third time. Alphonso was about to be married and, being in good humour, once more gave his consent to the appeals made on the wandering poet's behalf. It was hardly to be expected that the suppliant would be received with open arms after the treatment he had previously accorded his patron. The ministers and servants received him with indifference, some with open rudeness, and the family themselves were too much occupied with the wedding preparations and festivities to pay any attention to the

poet whatever. Angered at what he considered insult-
ing treatment, Tasso broke out into open revolt and
abuse of the whole D'Este family. This, coming to the
ears of the Duke, could have but one effect, his determination to place the disturber where he could be no
longer a source of annoyance, and Tasso found himself
a prisoner in the hospital asylum of St. Anna. Deep
and strong were the agonized cries of the caged bird
for freedom, but to no purpose. Pathetic and beautiful were the appeals he made in verse to both the Duke
and his sisters for his release but all went unnoticed
and were alike ineffectual. The same result followed
the entreaties made by influential personages of other
courts. The Duke was immovable and in this dungeon, though relieved occasionally by the mediation of
kind and influential friends and given now and then
short intervals of guarded liberty, the poet remained
for over seven years. It has been suggested that
Alphonso, fearing reprisal through the prisoner's pen,
or that Tasso, chafing under such long and degraded
captivity, might do him personal violence, was moved
to prolong the unfortunate poet's confinement. However this may be, on the fervent appeal of Gonzaga,
Prince of Mantua, who undertook to secure the Duke

TASSO.

against reprisal, Tasso left the confines of St. Anna's, a free, but broken-spirited man, in July, 1586.

Although a prisoner all these years his time had not been altogether wasted. Here he wrote his dialogue "The Father of A Family" and many verses of love and devotion to the two princesses, the younger and more beloved of whom, Leonora, did not long survive the incarceration of her faithful poetic admirer. How pathetically yet vividly does the great English bard who sang two and a half centuries afterwards, himself the sad and sorry victim of dejection, of passion, and of foiled ambition, express the feelings of poor Tasso while enduring all these tortures of long imprisonment and unrequited love:

> "They called me mad—and why?
> O Leonora wilt *thou* not reply?
> That thou wert beautiful and I not blind
> Hath been the sin which shuts me from mankind.
> But let them go, or torture as they will,
> My heart can multiply thine image still.
> Successful love may sate itself away,
> The wretched are the faithful—'tis their fate
> To have all feelings, save the one, decay
> And every passion into one dilate,
> As rapid rivers into ocean pour,
> And ours is fathomless and hath no shore.

. . . .

THE GREAT POETS OF ITALY.

Yes, Sister of my Sovereign! for thy sake
I weed all bitterness from out my breast.
It hath no business where *thou* art a guest.
Thy brother hates—but I can not detest.
Thou pitiest not—but I can not forsake.
I found the thing I sought—and that was thee,
And then I lost my being, all to be
Absorbed in thine—the world was passed away.
Thou didst annihilate the earth to me,
And thou Leonora! Thou who wert ashamed
That such as I could love, who blushed to hear
To less than monarchs that thou couldst be dear,
Go tell thy brother that my heart untamed
Adores thee still; and add—that when the towers
And battlements which guard his joyous hours
Of banquet, dance and revel are forgot,
Or left untended in a dull repose,
This, this shall be a consecrated spot!
No power in death can tear our names apart
As none in life could rend thee from my heart.
Yes Leonora! it shall be our fate
To be entwined forever—but too late."

Tasso's efforts, too, while a prisoner at St. Anna's
had been bent towards the amelioration of the wrongs
inflicted on him by the publication during his confinement of his " Jerusalem Delivered " by Malaspina and

154

others. While he derived no pecuniary benefit from this surreptitious exposure and sale of the best effort of his genius it yet brought him a large measure of fame, better attention in his incarceration, and visits and presents from influential, learned and well wishing personages. In 1582 his " Rime " was published and between this year and the date of his obtaining his freedom he watched calmly from his cell at St. Anna and ably defended himself in the great controversy which arose throughout all Italy between the Della Cruscan school, who championed the works of Ariosto, as against those who upheld Tasso, although the latter never denied that he had been inspired by Ariosto's works.

He went with his liberator to Mantua in 1586 and for a time enjoyed a respite from all the cares and bitter remembrances of the past. No one could have shown a broken-hearted man greater attention and kindness than the distinguished Mantuan bestowed on Tasso. He again visited Naples and Rome and though inducements were held out to him to join the Neapolitan Court he preferred to retire to the Monastery of Mount Oliveto. There, in the companionship of his young friend and future biographer Manso (afterwards the friend of Milton) at the latter's elegant palace and garden near Naples, the time passed pleasantly though marred by occasional outbreaks of melancholy and hallucination on Tasso's part. Stories are also told how about this time he lowered himself by composing, for any one that desired it, any kind of flattery for money or other sordid consideration.

In 1589 he visited the Monastery of St. Maria Nuova at Rome, where he remained several months and afterwards enjoyed a sojourn at the Tuscan court where many distinguished marks of favour were bestowed upon him by the greatest of the Florentines. Returning again to Naples in 1592 he found opportunity to complete his " Conquest of Jerusalem " which he had begun as a sort of sequel to, or perhaps more properly a correction or revision of, his " Jerusalem Delivered." This work never equalled the former in popularity although its author always claimed more merit for it than its predecessor. Having eliminated every word in praise of the Estensi from it, and having dedicated this last work to Cardinal Cinthio, a nephew of Pope Clement the Eighth, Tasso now received a papal invitation to Rome which he accepted. Notwithstanding his Ulysses-like habit of wandering from place to place and never being long satisfied, he would most likely have remained there had not inroads upon his health induced him to return to Naples. Tasso always seemed to think, like Virgil long before him, that Naples agreed better with his health than Rome. But the influences and attractions of the papal court proved too strong an allurement, coupled as they were with the promise of a public coronation in the Capitol. Since Petrarch's time this honour had been conferred on no Italian poet, so in spite of his ill health Tasso, still ambitious of worldly fame, entered Rome in pomp in November, 1594. Not only the highest honour, but pecuniary advancement and ease, seemed to come to him now all at once. A pension from the pope awaited him and the prince Avellino, who was in possession of his maternal estate, agreed to allow him an annual rent charge which would make him independent.

Owing to unseasonable weather the coronation was postponed till the spring, but this final triumph and honour the great poet was not destined to see, nor was he to benefit long from his improved financial condition. Feeling a return of his disorder and that his end was near, he received permission from his illustrious friends to retire to the Convent of St. Onifrio, on the hillside of the Janiculum, where he died on April 25th, 1594. From his lips, as his soul took its departure, were uttered the well-known words of Psalm xxxi, verse 6, which have soothed the dying moments of so many fervent believers, beginning:

"In Manus Tuas Domine."

Near the Convent door may still be seen the gnarled old oak where Tasso often reclined during his illness and from which he viewed the beauties and contemplated the past glories of the Eternal City.

Like many other illustrious men who have followed poetry and letters Tasso received after death far greater honour and homage than was ever accorded him in life. All Rome rang with his praise and his renown. The laurel and the toga, which were not to be his in life, adorned his remains as they were borne by torchlight through the streets of Rome and an elegant monument, though after eight years of delay, was erected in the Church of St. Onifrio, not by his friend Cinthio who had promised it, but by the Cardinal Boniface Bevilacqua of Ferrara. But Tasso's works had made all other monuments superfluous. If he has to give place to any epic poet before or after him the only

TASSO.

three are Homer, who perhaps excels Tasso in simplicity and fire; Virgil, to whom he may have to yield the palm in tenderness (though Mr. Wiffen, in one of the copious notes to his admirable translation, declines even in the teeth of such authorities as Boileau and Addison, to yield the palm to Virgil in any single particular) and Milton, who may rank higher than Ferrara's bard in sublimity. Tasso certainly leads both Virgil and Milton in at least one great point, that of continuity of interest and episode. With the beautifully-told story of the " Jerusalem Delivered " it may be said, as with the divine Homer, that it maintains its interest to the last and that, unlike the long poems of Spenser and Ariosto, there is nothing tedious in the Story of the Crusade. Even the great German Goethe has paid Tasso magnificent tribute in the lyric drama named after him.

He is the poet who first introduces sentiment into his verse and it is this refined feeling for woman which breathes throughout all his episodes in the " Jerusalem Delivered " and the life-like portrayal of the noble exploits and sacrifices of the converted pagan heroines of the story which, more than anything else, give it its unquestioned place as the first epic of mediæval or

THE GREAT POETS OF ITALY.

modern Italy. What can surpass in pathos, in remorse or in graceful melancholy this description of the duel between the lovers Tancred and Clorinda and the baptism of the latter by the former ere she yields her last expiring breath. I quote from Mr. Wiffen's Spenserian translation:

But now, alas, the fatal hour arrives
That must shut up Clorinda's life in shade;
In her fair bosom deep his sword he drives;
'Tis done—life's purple fountain bathes the blade!
The golden-flower'd cymar of light brocade,
That swathed so tenderly her breasts of snow,
Is steep'd in the warm stream: the hapless maid
Feels her end nigh; her knees their strength forego;
And her enfeebled frame droops languishing and low.

He, following up the thrust with taunting cries,
Lays the pierced Virgin at his careless feet;
She, as she falls, in mournful tones outsighs,
Her last faint words, pathetically sweet;
Which a new spirit prompts, a spirit replete
With charity, and faith, and hope serene,
Sent dove-like down from God's pure mercy-seat,
Who, though through life his rebel she had been,
Would have her die a fond, repentant Magdalene.

TASSO.

"Friend thou hast won; I pardon thee, and O
Forgive thou me! I fear not for this clay,
But my dark soul—pray for it; and bestow
The sacred rite that laves all stains away:"
Like dying hymns heard far at close of day,
Sounding I know not what in the sooth'd ear
Of sweetest sadness, the faint words make way
To his fierce heart, and, touch'd with grief sincere,
Streams from his pitying eye th' involuntary tear.

Not distant, gushing from the rocks, a rill
Clash'd on his ear; to this with eager pace
He speeds—his hollow casque the waters fill—
And back he hurries to the deed of grace;
His hands as aspens tremble, while they raise
The lock'd aventayle of the unknown knight;—
God, for thy mercy; 'tis her angel face!
Aghast and thunderstruck, he loathes the light;
Ah, knowledge best unknown! ah, too distracting sight.

Yet still he lived; and, must'ring all his powers
To the sad task, restrain'd each wild lament,
Fain to redeem by those baptismal showers
The life his sword bereft; while thus intent
The hallowing words he spoke, with ravishment
Her face transfigured shone, and half apart
Her bland lips shed a lively smile that sent
This silent speech in sunshine to his heart:
"Heaven gleams; in blissful peace behold thy friend depart!"

THE GREAT POETS OF ITALY.

A paleness beauteous as the lily's mix'd
With the sweet violet's, like a gust of wind
Flits o'er her face; her eyes on Heaven are fix'd,
And Heaven on her returns its looks as kind:
Speak she can not; but her cold hand, declined,
In pledge of peace on Tancred she bestows;
And to her fate thus tenderly resign'd,
In her meek beauty she expires, and shows
But as a smiling saint indulging soft repose.

It has been suggested that the author in this pathetic
description of the baptism and death of Clorinda at
the hands of Tancred intended to personify himself and
Leonora D'Este, the latter having died from grief at the
exposure of her love for the poet. That Tasso copied
from other poets, especially from Virgil, has never
been disputed but he had his own inimitable method
of portrayal. His personages are living portraits and
like those of Homer and of Shakspeare there is no
sameness, his whole poem abounds in variety of character and incident.

Torquato Tasso, we are told, was a man of large
stature, of fair but pallid complexion. His hair was
brown, his eyebrows black, his eyes of a vivid blue,
his nose and mouth both large. He had all those

162

attractions so winning with the beautiful women of his time—bodily strength, charming manners, varied accomplishments and open disposition. Strength, beauty, genius, purity and honour all were his. His voice was clear though his conversation was slow and impressive. His character was above reproach, he was faithful, candid, courteous and frank, patient in misfortune and pure in life and conduct. He was simple in his dress and preferred retirement to the noise and bustle of the world. His intellectual endowments were vast and his great ambition, the attainment of which was fully vouchsafed to him, was to excel in poetry. Had Tasso been granted a longer life than his comparatively limited space of fifty-one years it is hard to estimate to what greater heights in philosophy as well as poetry he might have attained, for the mental capacity to accomplish almost everything the human mind can embrace was surely his. Suffice it to say that he lived long enough to stamp on the poetry of Italy a delicacy and elevation of tone not found in the works of Dante and lacking also in Boccaccio and Ariosto. Like his master, Virgil, he knew how and when to suppress the unseemly and the vulgar both in word and thought. "Jerusalem Delivered" with its chief hero Godfrey De Bouillon, and its noble and melodious verse is a work abounding and continuing in purity of conception and loftiness of Christian effort. It marked the close of a line of manly and firm Italian poetry which was unfortunately to give place for a long period to the weaker and nerveless pastoral efforts, imitative but nowise the equal of Tasso's "Aminta" which came from the pens of Guarini, Marini and Tassoni and their ambitious but comparatively placid and feeble successors. Unmercifully assailed by his enemies and rivals, Tasso's high character and piety prevented the accomplishment of their efforts to soil his good name, though his life of mingled glory and sorrow was one of the saddest that it is the biographer's task to tell, of one of the world's most dazzlingly brilliant men.

In an age highly venal and degenerate, that piety, too, enabled him to surmount the many temptations open to him to a life of worldliness and corruption and to accept cheerfully the darkness of his fate "as night, which, though hiding the charms of the world, does but reveal the beauties of the sky."

TASSO.

TO TASSO.

I.

Torquato! in whose person rose
  The pride of old Bergamo's line
Ambition's triumphs, failure's woes,
  Glory and sorrow, both were thine.

II.

The darling of a ducal court
  The life of Leonora's bower
Condemned with madmen to consort
  In weird St. Anna's gloom to cower!

III.

There seven sad and fretful years
  For thee their weary cycles ran,
Unheard thy murmurings, thy tears
  Unheeded till the Mantuan

IV.

Gonzaga, generous prince and mild,
  With cruel D'Este fervent pleaded
Who, scorning to be reconciled,
  Yet now thy prayer for freedom heeded.

165

THE GREAT POETS OF ITALY.

V.

Yet even there thy pen could tell
  The story of the great crusade,
Though heavier still the blow that fell
  When pirate hands on it were laid.

VI.

And others reaped what thou hadst sown
  The fruit of many a toiling year
The tale of brave De Bouillon
  The Cross's bold gonfaloniere.

VII.

O bard divine, was't despite cold,
  Was't love unanswered made thee roam
And, like Ulysses, face the wold
  The prince of song without a home?

VIII.

Did Leonora rend thy heart
  With weak response or greeting chill;
Or did thy foiled ambition smart
  'Neath some unseen yet greater ill?

TASSO.

IX.

Which made thy burdened spirit break
  Beneath its load of gathering woe,
And drove thee sanctuary to make
  The precincts of Onifrio?

X.

Sorrento! thou gav'st Tasso birth.
  Ferrara! thou his woes began.
Rome! thou thy papal pomp put forth
  To crown the great Ausonian!

XI.

But death stepped in, no not for him
  Clement's and Cinthio's fading bays.
A laurel his which doth not dim
  But brightens with the length of days!

XII.

No sculptor's art could e'er augment,
  No garland add to his renown.
His works his noblest monument
  His poetry a deathless crown!

VITTORIO ALFIERI.

PART VI.

ALFIERI

ALFIERI

---

*Vittorio Alfieri, born at Asti in Piedmont, January 17th,
1749. Died at Florence, October 8th, 1803.*

IT IS a far cry both in point of time and in the nature
of what they accomplished for Italian poetry and letters from Ariosto and Tasso to Alfieri—from the
smooth flowing cadence, the mellifluous and easy style,
the varied wit and humour of the gentle poet of
Reggio and from the stanzas of the serious, melancholy, ideal-seeking author of the " Gerusalemme
Liberata " each in his turn in the 16th century the
slave and the tool of the lords of Ferrara, to the fiery,
impulsive, ungovernable reviver of Italian dramatic
art, born of a wealthy and noble Piedmontese family
at Asti in 1749.

During this hiatus of about two centuries Italian
poetry and in fact all Italian literature had sunk to a
very low ebb. True, the great literary chasm had been

bridged over in a kind of way but the structure was weak, imitative and artificial. Guarini had contributed his " Pastor Fido," a pastoral abounding in immoralities and largely copied from the ancients. The tonsured Tassoni had produced a witty and interesting but far-fetched and coarse mock-heroic entitled " The Rape of the Bucket " founded on some incidents of the Italian Civil Wars of the 13th century and had attempted by his satirical thrusts to add a little animation and virility to his country's quickly-decaying verse. Filicaja, the aristocratic Florentine Della Cruscan, who appeared like a small oasis upon this poetic desert in 1642, wrote an occasional patriotic sonnet and enlivened the torpidity of his surroundings for a brief period by his stirring " Odes to Victory " after the King of Poland had hurled the encroaching Turks from the ramparts of Vienna. Metastasio, the son of the Italian peasant Trapassi, had secured for himself and his country a certain measure of fame in the field of lyric and drama but he had retired early in life to Vienna and his best efforts can hardly be credited to Italian poetry. Casti, who had travelled with foreign embassies to nearly all the famous courts of his day and had been a close observer of the

intrigues which were usually indulged in by royalty
and those in attendance on it, had unmercifully flayed
and exposed in his mock heroic " The Talking Beasts "
the shams, the treachery and the ingratitude of kings
and those occupying the seats of the mighty, the places
of emolument and power. But the wars of the Spanish
Succession had involved nearly all the provinces of
the Italian peninsula, whose sovereignties were being
continually bartered and exchanged without the least
attempt to consult or consider the wishes of their
peoples. The new rulers oppressed and debauched
the territories of which they were supposed to be the
governors and protectors. Lettered and scholarly men
felt that under the tyranny of Spanish dominion there
was nothing of high national art or of culture worth
the striving for.

The period of the " Secentismo " headed by Marini,
with all its artificialities and conceits, with all its Della
Cruscan dissections and ramifications, had been followed by a school of poetry of an exactly opposite and
reactionary line of thought, that of the Arcadians, with
their feeble and puerile simplicities. Each had contributed to the impoverishment and exhaustion of
Italian verse, both lyric and dramatic; the former by

its bombast, its fantastic details, its pretty trifles, the latter by its pettiness and its effeminacy.

Galileo, though in prose, was the first contributor to a new and higher order of things in Italian literature, combatting as he did with his precise and easy and elegant style and diction the excessive rhetorical ornateness of the first of these two schools of poetic expression and the weakness and artlessness of the second. Then came Parini, with his onslaughts against the existing self-indulgences and trifles of the times. As a caustic satirist he exposed, in plain but delicate irony, the frivolities and futilities of the degenerate aristocracy of his day. And while Parini was indulging in these flights of satire the Venetian Goldoni was laying the foundation for dramatic reform by introducing on the Italian stage the comedy of character instead of that of imitation. So that it may be conceded that the inventive originality of these three men Galileo, Parini, Goldoni, each in his separate field, nurtured and encouraged by a feeling of love of liberty and equality akin to that which was at the same time sowing and fostering the seeds of revolution in France, was gradually leading to a popular demand for a new Italy and an awakening civilization. To this intellectual revival

174

built upon the ancient literature and the patriotism of their country the dash and brilliancy of Alfieri and the genius of himself and those who immediately followed him were to add the superstructure and to bring to fruition the good seed that the three earlier workers had planted and watered so well.

Vittorio Alfieri was a great traveller and no sooner had he broken away from his school at Turin, which he did at fourteen, than he, with a tutor and a train of servants (for he was rich, having inherited by this time a vast landed property with its retinue of domestics) visited nearly all the large Italian cities. His tour did him little or no intellectual good however, for having declined to accept any more than the most rudimentary education, he knew nothing of the dialects spoken at the different places he visited, nor of cultured Italian itself. His home tongue was a local patois, the only other language he attempted being very indifferent French. But it seemed that so long as he could get away from the old-fashioned restraints and the annoying and confining conventionalities of his Piedmontese home it was all he wanted. So he started again almost immediately after returning from his Italian tour, on this occasion unattended, and with

THE GREAT POETS OF ITALY.

France, England and Holland as his objective points. This time, too, he had discernment enough to recognize his lack of education and knowledge of the languages and he determined before venturing on another journey to become better versed in at least the language and literature of his own country. He took up the works of the best Italian authors, both in prose and verse, and after devoting some time to these and to the study of the institutions of his own country, he determined to visit and enquire into conditions in far-off lands which Italians rarely reached, among them Sweden, Denmark, Russia and Prussia. Before returning home he also touched at Spain and Portugal, fought a duel with an English officer, Lord Ligonier, because of too close attentions to the latter's wife and returned to Turin only to become involved in another amour, this time with the Marchesa Turinetti di Prie. But it is said that he had to thank this latter escapade for first turning him to the great afterwork of his life— tragedy. Idling away the time one day in the boudoir of his then indisposed mistress, he picked up some waste sheets of paper and seeing on some of the tapestries in the room scenes from the lives of Antony and Cleopatra, he dreamily and carelessly wrote the

176

skeleton of what was afterwards to be his famous tragedy called after the Egyptian Queen. Disturbed in the middle of his reverie, he hurriedly tucked the scraps of paper under the sofa, and did not see them again till over a year afterward when he sought and found them to add to and complete what he had already sketched from the many fresh thoughts and incidents that had sprung into birth in his imaginative mind in the long interval. Although its author thought much of this work at the time and devoted great care to its completion and it was successfully presented to the public at Turin, he grew to dislike it in after life when composing other and what he thought more creditable pieces and did not publish "Cleopatra" among his authorized works. Its chief defect seems to have been the unhistoric characterizing of his heroine. Instead of painting her as queenly, dignified, bewitching and clever, as Plutarch and Shakspeare have done, he depicts the temptress of Antony as cunning, spiteful and absolutely foolish. But this play it was, questionable as may have been its real merits and success, and however lacking in historic accuracy, that decided Alfieri to pin his reputation to tragedic effort. With what measure of success his country and the world at large now know!

THE GREAT POETS OF ITALY.

He felt that he was sorely lacking in scholarship even yet and at thirty years of age began what most school-boys start, a course of grammar and poetry in both the Latin and pure Italian tongues at Sienna, which at that time was regarded as the most cultured and advanced seat of Italian letters. Here he wrote fourteen of his tragedies. While studying at Sienna he visited Rome for a brief respite from work and here met Louisa von Stolberg, otherwise known as the Countess of Albany, the wife of Charles Edward Stuart, the English Pretender. An alliance sprang up between the two which only the death of the great tragedian-poet was to sever and which, notwithstanding the questionable character of some of its earlier incidents, made very largely for the comfort and happiness and steadying success of Alfieri's after life. The Pretender was nearly double his wife's age and having become by this time a poor besotted drunkard and an object of pity and ridicule to everyone, no companion for his wife or any other self-respecting woman, Louisa could hardly be blamed for seeking solace and companionship elsewhere. She and Alfieri soon found their admiration and love for each other's society mutual and permanent. A papal bull allowed the princess to live apart from her husband, and after his death shortly afterward she became the acknowledged wife of Alfieri. Following the lady of his heart from place to place, in turn to Alsace, to Paris and Florence, he filled up his time in the intervals by composing treatises, satires and sonnets beside six more of his favourite tragedies. He also translated Virgil, Sallust and Terrence and added five " Odes on the American Revolution " to his list of works. About this time, Alfieri, feeling his vast Piedmontese possessions more of a care than an advantage, and their management and supervision a drag on his literary ambitions and freedom, yielded them all up to his sister in consideration of a comparatively small annuity. There is nothing to show that he ever regretted this step and no doubt the fortune of his princess wife added to his own allowance was more than ample for both.

Alfieri was devoted to horseflesh and used to take long journeys to England and other far-off places for no other purpose than to add to his fine stud. On one occasion he led a large batch of horses personally across the Alps to Florence. I said in beginning that the poet, though nobly born, had early evinced a love

of freedom and a hatred of monarchical and other—
as he thought—despotic institutions. So when the
French Revolution broke out it was only natural that
his sympathies should go out to the unhappy French
peasantry in their fight against Bourbon tyranny and
one-man rule. He arrived in Paris just as the Revolution was breaking out and, as the English Wordsworth was doing about the same time, at first took a
sympathetic and active part against the monarchy.
But the horrors of the Jacobins, the assassinations and
cruelties of Marat and the other butchers of the time
drove Alfieri to the opposite extreme and caused him
to leave France again in 1792. His precipitate flight
brought about the confiscation of his property in Paris
and the sequestration of his books. His experience
in France seemed to turn him permanently against the
French, and all his writings from this on show this
antagonism. He had indeed written several works in
the cause of Liberty and against Monarchy which he
now, perhaps like a coward, took care to disavow and
to have suppressed.

After leaving France he settled down with the lady
of his choice at Florence to pass the rest of his days,
which alas, were not destined to be lengthy. He began

ALFIERI.

the study of Greek at forty-eight and the last six years of his life, outside of the time devoted to what must be admitted to be a very flattering autobiography, were given over to the acquiring of poetical and dramatic excellence in that ancient tongue. Alfieri died of the gout in October, 1803, attended to the last by his royal and faithful wife, who at great expense caused to be erected that glorious Canovan tomb so much admired by the tourist who visits Florence to-day, placed as it so appropriately is, in the Church of Santa Croce, between the resting places of the two greatest of Italians.

I need not refer in this brief summary to Alfieri's other poetical works outside of his tragedies. The latter are what he is chiefly, and indeed almost solely remembered by, and honoured for to-day in Italy. There is no decoration in his plays and none of the outside frills and flowery, unnatural descriptions usually tacked on to the works of other dramatists. In his efforts to adhere to the Aristotelian unities he hits out directly in harsh and abrupt, though clear and pure language, and in powerful delineation of dramatic character. His subjects are taken from both Ancient and Modern history, from Mythology and from Scripture. His action is never complicated. He does not encumber his plays with a confusing number of characters, nor are the scenes spun out to include a great period of time. His theme is usually the cruelty of tyrants, their love of crushing out the weak and their overbearing display of arbitrary power. None of his plots are original. His stories taken from fable and mythology had mostly been treated of before by the ancient classic dramatists. But the activity and sprightliness of mind of the Italian tragedian and his ability to give a natural and life-like portrayal to all his characters enabled him, in spite of his lack of originality, to leave his country many tragic compositions that have survived the onslaughts of time.

There is much difference of opinion on the varying merits of Alfieri's tragedies. His first works are not, generally speaking, regarded, either in literary merit or in portrayal of realistic character, as equal to his later productions. Harshness and excessive plainness seem to somewhat mar the former. It is doubtful whether he ever improved on his Biblical tragedy of " Saul " which appeared about the middle period of Alfieri's renown as a dramatist. The reason for this may be that the simplicity of the Israelitish surroundings fitted in with the naturally unadorned word portrayals of the dramatist. Lord Macaulay is high in his praise of this work as a poem. Next to Saul the tragedies most true to real life and exhibiting most powerfully the dramatic character are " Myrrha," " Mary Stuart," " Polonice " and " Philip II." One needs only to peruse the first-named of these to get an idea of the wonderful constructive and imaginative gift which Alfieri possessed. Taking the plot of Ovid—prurient and unnatural at its best, too immodest by far for decent ears to hear or eyes to behold, as its original author tells the story—he completely transforms the horrible details of the ancient classic into a proper and natural narrative, yet leaving in it all those pathetic and agonizingly-human features so essential to real tragedy. His play of Brutus, though strong, departs too much from the actual records of history to be really meritorious.

But in any event the firm and manly stand Alfieri took in combatting the languid and prosaic dramatic dialogues of his day and his successful efforts to overcome the prevalent degradation of tragic taste caused him to be hailed and rightly so as the great, in fact the sole, Italian tragic poet of his time.

THE GREAT POETS OF ITALY.

How like our own impetuous and brilliant Byron was the great dramatist of Piedmont! The versatile biographer could draw comparisons almost *ad infinitum* between these two, but a few of them will suffice here. Both aimed to excel in dramatic art and while the Englishman was perhaps too egotistical to ever be a great dramatist and too prone to picture himself as the hero of his own plays, he, like his Italian precursor of half a century, strove in all his stage productions to adhere to the Aristotelian unities of time, place and action. The chief aim of Alfieri and one of those of Byron was the elevation of the tragic stage. Both were of noble birth, both losing their sires in infancy and becoming petted and spoiled in youth, refused to learn at school or to become amenable to discipline. Both squandered a glorious patrimony. Both fell easy victims to the baser sort of female charms and the lives of both are marred with stories of wronged husbands and the impulses and intrigues of sensual passion. Both were fond of horses and of adventure. Both rebels against law and order, were erratic in the extreme, and galling under domestic restraint, wandered from home and country. Neither seemed as if they could ever be satisfied with what the life that suited the majority of mankind had to give. The sublime and the melancholy fitted to the disposition of each and both hated and fretted under the chafing bonds and the artificial restraints of society. Both longed and sought for a condition of affairs where government would be freer, sentiment more elevated, friendship deeper and love more devoted. Both had a defiant and exalted idea of their own importance. Both born aristocrats, soon embraced the spirit of freedom and revolution which in their time was sweeping over Europe and calling the most adventuresome and restless spirits of all lands to serve under its banner. And if their lives and early activities were so much alike, how equally did the charms of Hellas call to both in their latter years, though in entirely different ways? The great Englishman, though coming long after, died much the earlier in life of the two, actively in arms and engaged to the last in his efforts to free the Ancient and Classic peninsula from the Turkish yoke. The Italian, though dying peacefully on the banks of the Arno, occupied nearly all the last six years of his life in the study of the poetry and drama of Greece, in translations from her tongue and in the composition of comedies, tragedies and satires from the treasure house of her rich and marvellous mythology.

THE GREAT POETS OF ITALY.

TO ALFIERI.

I.

In that dark age when aught of life or worth
   From out Italian poetry was shorn,
When false dramatic taste had sprung to birth
   And tragedy was dead with none to mourn,
Came forth at Asti, he who was to free
His country's stage from lifeless pedantry.

II.

The curse of Spanish sovereignty was rife,
   Marini's poor conceits were ebbing low.
Old and unreal heroes without life
   Weighted the bombast of " Secentismo,"
And Della Cruscan nicety of dress
Had turned to weak Arcadian pettiness.

III.

True, Guarini's pastorals had told
   Poor mimic tales of loves and treacheries;
Tassoni, how Modena strove to hold
   The bucket stolen from the Bolognese,
And Filicaja's Odes extolled the work
Sobieski did in hurling back the Turk.

186

ALFIERI.

IV.

Melodious Metastasio at least
   Had won renown in operatic plays,
And Casti, in his realm of bird and beast,
   Had told in allegoric witty ways
In mock heroic, what deceiving curs
Were Kings and ministers and courtiers.

V.

But 'twas Galileo who first corrected
   These weak, effeminate styles in flowing prose.
Goldoni who false comedy detected
   And strove its imitations to expose,
Who banished from the stage its mocking blurs
And ushered in comedic characters.

VI.

Parini too, in caustic irony
   Had dealt voluptuousness a mortal blow;
And ease and trifling and frivolity
   Before his withering scorn had trembled low.
How well these three had tilled the wasted field
Alfieri sowed! How plentiful its yield!

THE GREAT POETS OF ITALY.

VII.

Panting for freedom, seeking the sublime,
    His youth misspent in unattained desire,
A wanderer through many a distant clime,
    The language of his country yet to acquire.
'Twas only at life's noon Alfieri came
To thirst for drama and tragedic fame.

VIII.

Then 'neath his drastic mind and pen there fell
    The chanted langours of the Tuscan lyre.
His rugged trenchant diction rang the knell
    Of tedious stage prosaists, lifted higher
The tragic art, to breathe in Grecian mould
The freedom of the Athenian bards of old.

IX.

How well he conquered unseen difficulties,
    His clear cut tragedies must ever tell;
Culled from both old and modern histories
    And Scripture and mediæval lore as well,
And, as if needing mightier triumphs, he
Explores the realms of Greek mythology.

ALFIERI.

X.

See Cecri plead with Venus to approve
   Myrrha's betrothal to Epirus' King!
See portents dread presaging from above
   The goddess' wrath at the unholy thing!
How chivalric the bridegroom's sore distress!
How genuine Ciniro's bitterness!

XI.

Lo Israel! trembling on Gilboa's heights,
   The Philistines advancing all around,
The gloomy king each stir and sound affrights
   For Endor's witcheries and sprites abound!
Hark! how the tuneful David strives to call
From destiny's dark doom unhappy Saul!

XII.

Watch Royal Philip! Moody jealous one,
   In league with the inquisitor of Spain,
Condemn to death his inoffensive son,
   Hear Isabella supplicate in vain!
Thus strips he off the masks of time and place
And brings real human creatures face to face.

THE GREAT POETS OF ITALY.

XIII.

How like to Newstead's bard in various ways
   Was Alfieri! passionate yet brave,
A hater of convention all his days.
   To female wiles and blandishments a slave.
Both born 'mid tottering thrones and wars alarms,
Both titled, drinking deep of freedom's charms.

XIV.

Each lost his sire ere well his youthful mind
   Had learned obedience or discipline.
Each loved to wander far from his own kind.
   Self will and pride swayed each and each was vain.
Each gloried in factitious self display.
Each threw a noble patrimony away.

XV.

Each sought a clime of Government more free,
   Of thought uplifted to a higher plane
Than Albion gave or ruled in Italy,
   Where social barriers could not restrain,
Of deeper friendship, love more seeming true,
Than their domestic firesides ever knew.

ALFIERI.

XVI.

And in their deaths 'twas Homer's land that called
   Her cry of war and art and song to each.
One strove to break her Turkish yoke that galled;
   The other with her Muse his mind to teach.
And Florence saw him pass away in peace
Mellowed and chastened by the lore of Greece.

XVII.

In Santa Croce's ancient lordly pile,
   Where lie the bones of many mighty men,
Where art enriches every niche and aisle,
   Thou sleepest! Piedmont's gifted citizen!
Well guarded there thine ashes and thy bust,
'Twixt Angelo's and Machiavelli's dust.

XVIII.

There she who left for thee a princely line
   And saw on thee bestowed in thy last days
Those honours due the noblest Florentine,
   Reared thee a stately tomb which best displays
Canova's art. There thy medallion
The admiring world to-day may gaze upon.

THE GREAT POETS OF ITALY.

XIX.

But Alfieri, though a thousand eyes
   Press daily toward thy tomb down Croce's nave,
Though Stolberg's lavish outlay beautifies
   The best Passagno's sculptor ever gave;
Thy land remembers thee to-day far more
That thou her lifeless drama didst restore.

XX.

Sleep on then, Asti's bard! That ornate tomb
   Well fits thee—to the rich and splendid born
The fiery pulse and untamed will of whom
   Such rare sepulchral trappings well adorn.
Thou strenuous toiled, thou gav'st the land thy best,
Sleep on amid the great and take thy rest!

GIACOMO LEOPARDI.

PART VII.

LEOPARDI

LEOPARDI

Giacomo Leopardi, born at Recanati, June 29th, 1798.
Died at Capodimonte, June 14th, 1837.

I AM concluding this work, or rather this branch of a more extensive one, which with time and opportunity vouchsafed, I hope some day to complete, by a sketch of the career of one of the most brilliant, but withal the saddest and most unfortunate of beings, who ever contributed to the literature of any land or time. Poverty has been the lot of many of the world's best poets and in numerous instances they have struggled manfully and successfully against it, and, defying its chilling blasts, have attained fame. But in spite of the assertions of philosophers and saints to the contrary, there is no doubt that the thoughtful and imaginative soul who is surrounded with at least the comforts and necessaries of life, who has been carefully trained and instructed in youth, who can enjoy ease and luxury,

195

reading and travel, who can relieve the monotony of life by diversity of scene and change of companionship, that man, whether it be in the exuberance of youth, the confidence of middle age, or in the calm of life's eventide, has a long advantage over others with the same natural gifts but not so fortunately placed in the world. Opportunities are most assuredly presented to him to bring to perfection in form and in thought any native poetic genius with which it may have been his rare good fortune to be endowed, far and away above those of the individual whose hard lot has vouchsafed him none of these benefits. Who would be rash enough to suggest that Petrarch or Tasso or Alfieri could ever have brought their works and attainments to the high plane of success which they did, had they not taken advantage of the luxurious and splendid surroundings and that intercourse with the renowned and the great which the youth of each offered to these famous Italian poets? The choice writings of Addison and of Pope were largely conceived and dictated by the style of the company they kept, the manners and habits of those they associated with and the ease and refinement of their surroundings. So were the satires and witticisms of Swift. Byron drew most of both his lyric and dramatic inspiration, not from poverty and squalor, but from scenes of high life, from the doings and actions of those who inhabited the court and the palace. Rogers' best productions were planned from his travels in Italy and other places where knighthood and chivalry held sway and from his intermingling with persons and things socially above him. The best thoughts of Tennyson were more or less gathered from scenes and incidents in the high and exalted rather than in the lower walks of life. Thus I could go on and give other instances in all ages and countries where poverty has retarded, and opportunity in the form of either wealth or social prominence, or both, has developed and brought to the highest fruition the poetic gift in man. And if the lack of material advantage has hindered so much this development and this perfection what must we say of the doubly unfortunate individual who, possessing to a wonderful extent the scholarly and the poetic genius, has not only to fight all his life against want, who has no pecuniary assistance with which to obtain those things I have just mentioned that can mellow and refine and enlarge and broaden his natural gifts, but who has also to battle all the time against disease and whose dim light of life is liable momentarily to be snuffed out by those trifling attacks of indisposition which with most of us go almost unheeded? All countries have had similar instances in their literature and poetry of such sad cases of double affliction. Keats and Kirk-White are two striking examples of brilliant genius baffled and retarded by both ill health and want in our own literature. So too may be mentioned Chatterton and Savage and later on Hood, and English poetry has doubtless many other names of similar unfortunates.

Of such too, was Giacomo Leopardi, the early nineteenth century Italian poet of the romantic school of whom I am now attempting to write a brief memoir and who, through the fiery zeal on behalf of liberty displayed in his verse, came to occupy the foremost place among the group known as "the patriot poets" of his time. He was born at the quiet little town of Recanati in the Bolognese district on the 29th of June, 1798. The family was, like those from whom most of the great poets of Italy had sprung, a noble one but through the vicissitudes of fortune and the extravagance of its former heads it had sunk to such a condition of financial embarrassment as to make the title of "Count" of which Monaldo Leopardi, the future

poet's father, boasted, an empty and almost a ludicrous
one. The then holder, if he had ever taken any part
in the things of the world around him, by the time
his son Giacomo came upon the scene, had given up all
interest in the affairs of the nation and being fond of
reading and study had retired to the recesses of his
extensive library. Here he could dream away in soli-
tary sadness—he no doubt thought—those few years
that yet remained to him and reflect on the past glories
of his race undisturbed by the turmoils and passions
of social and political life, in neither of which he
now took any interest or professed any knowledge.
Giacomo's mother was a clever business woman but
as the cares of the family and the management of the
now impoverished estate were thrown entirely upon
her she had little time to devote to her clever son any
measure of that maternal affection which she may have
latently possessed. The boy, through stress of circumstances, spent most of his time in his father's library
and so it was not to be wondered at that he, too, early
became a bibliophile with a mind warped and narrowed
down to that little world which radiated from the
paternal bookshelves. But unlike the sire, there was in
the son that spark of genius and literary ambition

which learning and study were to kindle and finally to develop into a name and fame both for scholarship and poetry on a level almost with Dante and Petrarch and Tasso and the equal of which his country has, at least never since his time, produced. With no tutor and with no assistance outside of the grammar and the dictionary he had obtained at sixteen years of age a complete mastery of both the Latin and the Greek languages, not only in scholarship but also in his classical conception of life and in a knowledge of the antique in form and style. He was hardly any older when he wrote a history of astronomy, a treatise on the popular errors of the Ancients containing citations from over four hundred authors, and he had also now begun to turn to poetry in the form of Anacreontic odes.

How sad it was that while this wonderful advance in scholarship and letters was quietly but surely expanding the boy's physical growth and progress were being entirely neglected! But so it happened and when at eighteen young Leopardi produced his first great poem " The Approach of Death " his too close application to books and study had transformed him into a nervous wreck and into a sickly, stooped and quite deformed young man. In the " Appressa-

LEOPARDI.

mento alla Morte," lost for many years but afterwards discovered and published by Volta, may be seen the influence of both Dante and Petrarch, the first forming Leopardi's model, the other lending him his inspiration. And while the young Recanatian had not likely ever heard of Shelley although they lived and wrote almost concurrently,* a remarkable similarity in thought and outline exists in this work to the English poet's "Triumph of Life" in which the latter was engaged when Spezzia's billows claimed him as their prey. I quote three brief extracts from each poem or vision to show how closely allied must have been the thoughts of both these gifted young men though they were entire strangers to each other. These are from Leopardi's:

> "A rivulet poured forth its sweet lament,
> The sea shone in the distance and the fields
> And groves, and slowly rising one by one
> The summits of the mountains were revealed.
>
> . . . .
>
> The pattering rain drops falling fast were heard,
> The sound increasing as the cloud drew near,
> And round her now the glancing lightning flashed.
>
> . . . .

---

* Shelley was born eight years before the Italian and died too fifteen years before Leopardi.

THE GREAT POETS OF ITALY.

And folding close her clothes against her breast
She through the storm her fearful path pursued."*

And these from Shelley's:

"I was laid asleep
Under a mountain, which from unknown time
Had yawned into a cavern wide and deep,
And from it came a gentle rivulet
Whose water like clear air in its calm sweep
Bent the soft grass . . .

.   .   .   .

Till, like two clouds into one vale impelled
That shake the mountains when their lightnings mingle
And die in rain.

.   .   .   .

But among
The thickest billows of that living storm
I plunged and bared my bosom."

How like too is the expressed individual spirit of
dejection which sometimes enshrouded each: the

---

* The translation is that of Frederick Townsend, a lettered American born in New York but who spent much time in Italy. I found it
in the Chicago Public Library after a deal of vain effort in some of
our own best libraries. There is no name to the poem in Mr. Townsend's work. It is merely entitled "A Fragment" but Lacey Colli-
son Morley in his "Modern Italian Literature," p. 221, identifies it
as a part of the long-lost "Appressamento alla Morte." He goes on
to state there that this is the only fragment of Leopardi's early poems
that appeared in the final edition. None of the translators of Leopardi
into English that I can find seem to have undertaken the whole of this
poem and some of them have left out the fragment translated by
Townsend.

202

LEOPARDI.

gloomy young Italian lamenting his own fate and that of his country gives utterance to his feelings in these words:*

"Dark death for me no terrors hath in store,
  To-day but sport appears to me that which this world
  Of fools now praises, now abhors and fears,
  Life's last predestined bourne,
  Let danger come, I'm ready to confront
  Her every threat with smile of unconcern—"

while the expatriated Englishman, brooding one glorious noon over real or imagined ills as he sat on the shore of Naples' matchless bay, pours forth this sad soliloquy:

"I could lie down like a tired child
  And weep away the life of care
  Which I have borne and yet must bear
  Till death like sleep might steal on me."

Three years after he wrote "The Approach of Death," in spite of his physical drawbacks, young Leopardi surprised the literary world in which he moved by the production of two powerful political odes, one to Italy, the other on the monument to Dante at Florence. In both he exposes the deep degradation

---

* "My Sovereign Thought," Morrison's translation, p. 102.

203

in which he feels his country placed by the restoration
of tyranny and the throttling of freedom. Sadly in
these two famous odes does the poor, forlorn, ill-
shaped young bard of Recanati contemplate the political, intellectual and artistic impotence in which the
torpor of the last two centuries has landed his country.
In chaste but courageous language uninfluenced by
fancy, closely reasoned and without the usual ornaments of metaphor or hyperbole, with classic flavour-
ing yet permeated with the suggestion of the modern,
with a mingling of Landorian dignity and Byronic
passion—all till now new qualities in Italian poetry—
he deplores the manners and the times in which he
lives. Silently, all unnoticed, and yet surely is the
young poet in these denunciations paralleling his country's unhappy fate with that of his own life—broken,
disappointed, ruined! Nor did the wretched condition
of Italian literature escape his declamatory pen. The
discovery at the time by Cardinal Mai of some ancient
manuscripts furnished Leopardi with the opportunity
of lamenting in a third ode quite as fervid as the last
two the stagnation of Italy in letters as well as in
political and military glory.

Not content with the lasting interest, the profundity
and novelty of the themes upon which he writes, the

young poet reveals to the world in these impassioned productions the abandonment of the old conventional manner of Petrarch and all who had written since, and the adoption of an entirely new form and tone for those efforts, in which with clarion notes, he deplores the backslidings of his times.

His father, too closely wedded to the old order of things, could see nothing to admire in the new Shellian style and form and the classical Tuscan language of his clever son. When Giacomo, therefore, desired to leave the sedate and unambitious surroundings of his rural home in order to mingle with some of the learned minds of the capital, Leopardi senior was reluctant to encourage in his son what he thought a waste of both time and money. His correspondence about this time with the scholar and patriot Giordani shows how young Leopardi longed to flee from the morbidity and inertia of his home life to something more elevating and enlivening, where his learning and gifts might receive at least some little appreciation. Giordani had been drawn to the clever but downhearted youth and had tried to encourage him with his interest and his sympathy. However, the young poet managed to reach Rome in 1822 in spite of the aforesaid paternal objec-

tions and once there made the most of his opportunities by meeting and mingling with some of the best
scholars of his day. But letters and scholarship at this
period had long become enfeebled at the Eternal City
and Leopardi soon found that it took very little time
for a deep mind like his own to take in all the wisdom
and erudition that her so-called savants could impart.
His purse too, never a long one, had become depleted
so that he saw no alternative in front of him but to
return home. While at Rome he had also met some
distinguished German scholars and inducements were
held out to him by them to accept a lucrative position
in one of their highest seats of learning but this offer
the young poet for reasons not given had declined.
Had he been able to take orders he might have secured
public employment at Rome but his religious opinions
were unorthodox and at this time in the papal states
the Church formed the only avenue to the public service. Besides this, failing eyesight now gave him such
serious trouble that for months at a time he had to
abandon his studies altogether. At Recanati he found
that conditions were no more promising than formerly
although he did manage to bring out during the three
unhappy years in which he now remained at home

some masterful lyrics including " Bruto Minore," his
condensed philosophy of despair.

Leopardi moved to Bologna in 1825 and for a while
eked out a precarious existence there writing on philosophical subjects for a Milan publishing house. Shortly
after this, enlivened and entertained by the charms of
the Countess Malvezzi, he seems to have come out of
himself for a time and to have enjoyed a short respite
from the inroads of that pessimism and hypochondria
which usually enveloped him. He now appeared as a
prose writer and though his dialogues entitled "Oper-
ette Morale" are unreal and stilted and have very little
of merit in them but their form, in the latter they take
a very high place and in classicality of spirit, beauty of
construction and perfection of style, give their author
almost as high a place in modern prose as in poetry.
But poverty was again disturbing his plans and failing
any other refuge, the paternal roof at Recanati, poor
and dull and unattractive as it was, again appealed to
Leopardi. Once more returning home, he remained
there from 1829 to 1831, when by some turn of fortune he found himself in Florence. Here a Swiss
friend named Sinner undertook to disseminate and
spread abroad, more especially in Germany, the sickly

young poet's works. But though kind and encouraging
to his new friend, he sadly neglected and delayed the
commission he had undertaken so that while everything Leopardi wrote was received with the approba-
tion it deserved by the small circle whom the poems
reached he always felt that a much wider field of
admirers could have been his had the dilatory Sinner
but devoted more time and attention to what he had
taken in hand. However, a new edition of Leopardi's
works appeared in 1831 containing most of his best
efforts including " The Resurrection " and " The Song
of A Wandering Shepherd in Asia." The works
embraced in this volume seem too to have less in them
of austerity and of the wail of the pessimist, and display a more descriptive and generally a keener interest
in ordinary happenings and rise to higher flights than
any of the poet's former efforts.

A love affair shortly after this called Leopardi again
to Rome but there is no record of its ever having
ended in anything substantial or serious except the
appearance of a couple of short poems which indicated
deeply his own wounded pride and a lacerated heart.
Florence again claimed the poor, unsettled, deformed
poet for awhile and here his friendship for Ranieri,

the famous author, was formed. Shortly after meeting, the two went together to Naples to live. Here, devotedly watched over by Ranieri and the latter's sister, although still sorely afflicted in many ways, the poet spent more peacefully than ever before the last four years of his life. Ranieri afterwards made himself Leopardi's biographer but unfortunately tarnished the record of his many previous kindnesses towards the ill-fated young misanthrope of Recanati by making the biography more a record of his own accomplishments than of those of the dead poet. It was in Naples that Leopardi wrote his lyrical masterpiece "La Ginestra" (The Ginesta) and the famous satire after the form of Casti and in the manner of Homer's "Frogs and Mice" by which he is perhaps better remembered than in any of his other poems. In the latter he mercilessly portrays the hypocrisies and the unworthinesses of the foreign tyrants who were at the time misruling and debauching his native land. But the "Sequel to The Battle of The Frogs and Mice," though clever and caustic, is obscured, as far as the ordinary reader is concerned, by too many references to local and unknown characters.

Comparatively little more is to be recorded of the life and doings of this remarkable though short-lived

THE GREAT POETS OF ITALY.

Italian. It is not a stretch of the imagination to call his career a meteoric one, so brilliant was the dash he made across the literary firmament of his country, so revolutionary and amazing his style and form and so short the period in which his life-work was accomplished. He could not longer survive the inroads that disease and the buffetings of adverse fortune had brought upon him and died of dropsy at Naples early in 1837. His published works never made a large volume and at the time of his death all that had been then got together was very meagre indeed; there was only a mere fragment of the famous " Appressamento " then at hand, and its later discovery by Volta in complete form helped to swell the volume of new and unsurpassed verse which this gifted though ill-starred son of Italy left to posterity. Yet all told there are only a couple of score of Leopardi's poems extant which are worthy of the highest praise and some of these are mere fragments. His best efforts were in the form of odes but he also successfully adopted the soliloquy in some of his fervid appeals to the patriotism of his countrymen. His chosen form of expression was lyrical but he has also shown that he was no mean composer of blank verse.

LEOPARDI.

In another part of this work I have pointed out in how many ways the tragedian of Asti resembled Lord Byron. Leopardi, too, had many of the striking characteristics of the gifted author of "Childe Harold" and of "Don Juan." Like him he felt the absence of parental sympathy and love, was irritable and gloomy, dissatisfied with his lot, deformed in body, passionate and brilliant in his meteoric and revolutionary career and like him he filled an early grave. Similar too were their tendencies to wander, their hatred of tyranny, their love of freedom and the philosophy of their lives.

Leopardi may be called Italy's poet of pessimism rather than of hope and there is little surprise that this was so. Without the cheering and ennobling influences with which his great predecessors in song had been surrounded, bored by a dull and unattractive domestic fireside, with want and ill-health continually to contend with, it would have been nothing short of a miracle had he written in any other vein than the one he adopted. To him, too, the national future loomed up dark and foreboding. Split into petty provinces with factions both political and religious striving within and the heel of tyranny continually oppressing from without, with her beautiful cities pillaged of their treasure and much of her best territory wrested from her, there appeared to the serious and fretting youth of Recanati no light in the darkness ahead for Italy. Could he have peered three or four decades into the future and beheld a united and progressive country or could he have looked even further ahead and seen, as we now see, the land he loved so well joining with the other nations of Europe in the struggle against Teuton Militarism for world freedom how different might have been his whole view of life? Could he have only witnessed the present gigantic effort for the recovery from the grasping Hapsburgs of Italy's stolen possessions, his cry and his song in spite of his bodily afflictions, would doubtless have been like Filicaja's or Foscolo's or Manzoni's before him, one of hope and not of despair. How he would have rejoiced could he have read as we read to-day of his great successor in Italian poesy, Gabriele D'Annunzio, flying over Trieste and scattering from the clouds among the exiles there the greetings of their countrymen, wrapped in the white, red and green bunting of Italy, sure tokens of their early liberation and repatriation! How his hopes would have risen could he have lived to see falling from the same aircraft on the military buildings of Italy's hated foe those death-dealing bombs which were to warn grasping Austria that her hold upon those stolen possessions was nearly over!

But in spite of all this discouragement he played his part well. With a reverence for Dante and Petrarch and the old masters and an adherence to the beauties and classic sublimities of their writings he yet so changed by his originality of conception and concentrated energy of diction the whole form and thought of Italian verse that men woke on reading Leopardi's works to find themselves in a new literary era in which brighter and more modern methods of expression and construction had superseded the ancient and the effete. True, Foscolo, a score of years before Leopardi, had striven in his poetry to free himself from the old classical bondage of the past centuries. In a romantic vein he had written much that indicated a breaking away from the old models in both thought and construction. But disgusted with the efforts of himself and his compatriots to secure liberty for his country under the rule of Napoleon he had retired to England and may be said to have ceased in middle life his earlier efforts to rejuvenate Italian verse. What he had cautiously begun it was left to the afflicted but gifted Leopardi to drastically and thoroughly complete.

It cannot of course be asserted that Leopardi ever reached that fruition in descriptive charm, in invention, in high lyric flights, in perfection of form, in cleverness and humour, in those sparkling displays of wit and passion that English poetry was even then revealing in the productions of her great triumvirate. Nor had he attained to those heights that Scott and Coleridge or Wordsworth a little later on were to give utterance to or that the poetic world to-day experiences to the full in its best masters. In many of his works the critical reader can easily detect a limited range in the ideas of their author. But in nearly all Leopardi's poetry there can be easily observed at least an adumbration of all those future excellencies in verse which we enjoy to-day. Men beheld for the first time in him the consecrated spirit of the old, inspired and regenerated by the consummate literary skill, the power of observation, the unsurpassed style and melody of the new. As Alfieri half a century before had put new life and vigour into her artificial, slow-moving, decadent tragedy, so to Leopardi was it given to transform and rejuvenate the time-worn, mechanical framework of

LEOPARDI.

Italy's lyric poetry. To him then is due the lifting of Italian verse out of the rut of amatory and chivalric effusion in which for centuries past it had jogged along, into that livelier, more melodious, more natural channel and into that modern form and style which to a very large extent still governs it to-day.

THE GREAT POETS OF ITALY.

TO LEOPARDI.

I.

Like some spent meteor 'cross the starry sky
   Flashed Leopardi, friendless and alone,
Just to exist, and scintillate, and die,
   In conflict with himself and every one.
   He came, this fleeting pilgrim, and was gone,
This Hellenist in classicality,
   Who yet gave verse its modern form and tone,
Weakling and poor, and still whose fame should be
Such that his country venerates eternally.

II.

Italia! when thy future loomed up dark
   In nationhood, in letters, and in art,
When tyrants reigned, when Dante and Petrarch
   And all they stood for, had become the sport
   Of a base age and a corrupter heart,
A voice spake forth from Recanati's walls
   Destined new youth and impulse to impart
To thy old song, to reinspire those halls
Where pent-up freedom uttered her unheeded calls.

LEOPARDI.

III.

Dull was the place, and now alas! obscure,
  Though affluent once, the line that gave him birth
By failure forced those hardships to endure,
  Which banish ease and luxury and mirth,
  Parching the fountain springs of real worth,
And withering genius in its earliest bloom.
  From this decadent lineage sprang forth
Fretting and fettered, a soured soul from whom
There spake a wondrous mind beneath a load of gloom.

IV.

Wan and ill-formed, on whom disease had left
  Its hideous traces, on whom poverty
Continuous frowned, of every hope bereft,
  Groping for light 'mid dense obscurity,
  Could it be wondered that thy poetry,
O bard of Recanati, breathed despair,
  When all the woes of trampled Italy
Rose up before thee, weird and gaunt and bare,
With naught of future brightness radiating there.

THE GREAT POETS OF ITALY.

V.

How wretched, too, the home that nurtured thee,
  With everything to cloy and naught to please,
While others saw rare opportunity,
  Thy ruthless lot was not the lot of these.
  To strive with deafness, blindness, and disease,
And gnawing penury thy changeless fate
  Cursed with life's pains and its deformities
Thou lived'st, nor was it thine to know the great,
Nor mingle with the rich, the potentates of state.

VI.

Thou only saw in all thy country's woes
  The mirror of thine own benighted soul,
Her base betrayers, her intriguing foes
  Were as the vagaries of fate which stole
  Around thee like some mocking caracole;
And her discomfiture and gloom were thine.
  For thee, for her, there shone no cheering goal.
Thou with thine old but fast decaying line,
She smitten with the plague of tyranny's decline.

LEOPARDI.

VII.

That glorious land of the dim hoary past,
   That matchless, that unrivalled chronicler,
Of deeds of valour that through time will last,
   Of feats in art and letters that must stir
   Alike the breast of lord and villager.
Of her immortals how august the list!
   Scipios and Cæsars, mighty men of war!
Angelo! Raphael! names no years enmist!
Virgil, her prince of song! Horace, her satirist!

VIII.

How rich in legend, too, that native ground,
   Thou wept-for Leopardi! Ilia's sons
The she-wolf suckled, they whose forebear's wound
   Iapis healed, how those unmated ones
   The City's founders, like wild lustful Huns
Rushed on the Sabine maids, how daring lept
   Curtius to death, how safe Rome's legions
At Regillus the twins of Leda kept
Who wavering first, at length the foe before them
     swept.

219

THE GREAT POETS OF ITALY.

IX.

Soul piercingly her countless beauties too,
    Told thee O bard of what she once had been.
One cannot chide that still thou lovedst to woo
    This cypress-crowned, this ilex-mantled queen,
    Wisteria twined 'mid grape and olive sheen,
Her aqueducts and springs, her sacred pool,
    Egerian Clitumnus! Trasimene!
Nemi hill-nestling! Como deep and cool!
Nor griev'dst that with such lovely scenes she could
      not rule.

X.

But how thy genius lifted high her song
    Which Foscolo before thee tried to raise
Up from the dead antique which centuries long
    Had ruled her verse and amorous roundelays,
    Thou wrot'st in novel, sprightly, modern ways
Before unheard of, men woke to behold
    New style and form to their intense amaze.
In thy new phrase and in thy diction bold
A fresh poetic page yet reverencing the old.

220

LEOPARDI.

XI.

No wonder that thou couldst not tune thy lyre
   To happier flights when hope with thee was dead.
Thy native land too deep beneath the mire
   Of Hapsburg greed to raise her drooping head,
   The lustre of thy once proud household fled.
No wonder that the verse thy fancy wrote
   Was saturate with pessimistic dread.
For where hath poet sung in joyous note
With his own future dark, his Country's hopes remote.

XII.

True, there were bright spots in thy sad career.
   Kind Giordani heard and comforted,
And Sinner, though neglectful, gave thee cheer.
   With fair Malvezzi ill forebodings fled,
   The Ranieris gladdened thee and led
The way to Naples and thy day's decline,
   Consoled and solaced in its parting thread.
Thus Giacomo, 'mid thy soul's repine,
Some green oases in life's desert drear were thine.

221

THE GREAT POETS OF ITALY.

XIII.

Men liken thee to Byron in that he
  Was passionate and deformed, while others say
Thou sharedst with Landor in that dignity
  Which courted not the frivolous nor gay.
  To me far more than these, thy works display
The mind of him who passing early gave
  To English verse its best unchallenged day,
Who jested at the terrors of the grave,
And, singing of Life's triumph, sank 'neath Spezzia's
    wave.

XIV.

Who, soaring with his skylark, saw and told
  The unforbidden things of the Arcane,
The idealist who, deep peering, could behold
  Beyond the husk the soul's sublimer fane,
  Whose voice supreme in beauty and domain
Rose upward in poetic ecstasy
  Away above the things of the mundane.
The Shelley thou, of downcast Italy,
As kindly, generous, fickle and humane as he.

LEOPARDI.

XV.

O Leopardi! hadst thou lived to see
   Thy country reunited, cast the yoke,
Which chained her to her old servility,
   Couldst thou have breathed when Italy awoke
   To join the world in freedom's battle smoke,
To see her sons for liberty entrain
   To deal the Austrian line its lethal stroke,
How different then had been thy song's refrain,
How vanished thy despair, how glad thy muse's strain.

XVI.

Couldst thou have seen D'Annunzio from on high
   Scatter to those poor exiles in Trieste
That message which the flag of Italy
   Enfolded, how elate thy patriot breast,
   How quell'd that fretfulness and that unrest.
Couldst thou have known the grasping Hapsburg smote,
   Thy Country from th' encroaching tyrant wrest
Her stolen cities, o'er his bastions float
With her death-dealing bombs, how joyous then thy
     note.*

* On August 9, 1915, Gabriele D'Annunzio, Italy's foremost living poet, carried out his long-expressed intention of flying over Trieste and dropping from his aeroplane greetings to the Italian residents there, enfolded in the Italian flag. On the same flight bombs were dropped on the Austrian military buildings of the city. The poet's aeroplane was attacked by the enemy's air-craft, but returned in safety.

THE GREAT POETS OF ITALY.

XVII.

Yet, spite of all, thou playd'st a worthy part
  In that short life and in thy narrow sphere
And with rare skill and more consummate art
  Mad'st old forms and conventions disappear
  And a new energy and diction clear
In Italy's exhausted verse hold sway.
  'Twas given to thee, thou pilot bold, to steer
Thy country's poesy toward that higher way,
That more melodious path it journeys in to-day

PART VIII.

THE VISION OF DANTE

THE VISION OF DANTE

A Condensed Presentation in Rhyme of the
"Divine Comedy."

Se volete saper la vita mia
Studiando io sto lungi da tutti gli uomini,
Ed ho imparato più teologia
In questi giorni che ho riletto Dante
Che nelle scuole fatto io non avria.

(Demandest thou what things engross my mind
When loneliness' dark shadows hover o'er,
What consolation for the hours I find
When friends and kindred comfort me no more?
For sacred lore to Dante I repair
And find more wisdom than the Schoolmen's there.)*

Note.—My excuse for the many lapses and shortcomings of the following transposition is that it was hurriedly undertaken and composed as an after-thought to the rest of this

---

* The italicized stanza is my own perhaps-far-too-free rendering of the Italian lines by the learned Salvini quoted above it and which given literally read: "If you desire to know my life I am studying away from all men and in these days while reading Dante over again I have learned more theology than I should have done at college."

volume. It was entirely written during August, 1916, without the assistance of my library and in leisure moments while I was travelling about the country on other pursuits.

It will be observed that I have framed my account of Dante's tragic and fanciful wanderings through the spirit world in ten-lined rhyming heroic couplet stanzas, each concluding with an Alexandrine. This I thought would vary in a degree what some readers and critics of poetic form regard as monotonous in continued decasyllabic couplet verse. While Dryden approached this form by a frequent use of the Alexandrine in his " Translations from Boccaccio " and in the " Hind and Panther," I think the exact plan that I have adopted in my presentation of the Dantean Vision is new and experimental in English poetry and I trust its reception will not be an altogether unfavourable one. While the form I have chosen gives the same extended ending and final sweeping roll as the Spenserian stanza, it avoids the complicated rhyming plan of the latter that at first approach sometimes confuses the unfamiliar reader. I know that I may be accused of literary retrogression in adopting for my framework a form of versification so admittedly antique as the ten-syllable rhyming couplet. But in an age of flighty and unregulated rhyme and measure like ours, may not history, as in other things, repeat itself in poetry? Marlowe and Nash, and after these Milton, it will be remembered, carried literary England with them in their denunciation of this form and effectually superseded it with blank verse. But how wholly and universally, about a century later, did Dryden and Pope and Goldsmith, the first-named inspired by the harmonies of Edmund Waller, bring the English reading public back again from wild and unchecked stanzaic confusion to the worship of the polished and regular rhyming couplet! True, the school which this latter trio created and adorned, becoming too conventional,

THE VISION OF DANTE.

waned in its turn before the simpler and more attractive
nature lyrics of Cowper, Burns and Wordsworth and the lofty
and sensuous stanzaic flights of the other great triumvirate
of the Revolutionary Era. But since these mighty reformers,
what anarchy and discord have engulfed the rules of rhyme
and measure and verse at the hands of modern poetic
"plungers!" In poetry, as in the more sordid things, the
modern world may be truly said to have been "carried off its
feet" by reckless speculation and adventure and to have been
landed in a veritable ocean of degenerated prosody. Who for
example, accustomed to venerate or respect well established
and cherished forms of verse, can detect any poetic style or
harmony in free and commonplace stuff like the following
recently published as a sample of good up-to-date poetry and
given a prominent place and high praise in a leading New
York literary column:

" It's funny about tears:
  Once accidentally I broke a cup
  That I had kept a long while because it pleased my eyes
  With its delicate peacock blue colour,
  And I sobbed and sobbed
  As I looked at the scattered pieces
  And thought how they never could be quite the same again."

Facilis descensus Averni.—What a sorry departure this from
chasteness of expression, sublimity of thought, faultlessness of
measure and rhyme and all that go to make the artistic in the
courtship of the muse! So that when one considers the present
chaotic conditions in our rules of versification, or more strictly
speaking, the absence of any such rules at all, the idea easily
suggests itself that something worse might happen, especially in
the composition of continued poetic narrative, than a repetition

229

of what occurred in later Caroline and earlier Georgian times known as the classic period of our literature. Then it was that England's noblest bards, to escape the unbridled measures and the audacious and irregular flights of the romanticists, aptly termed by Saintsbury "the hideous jumble of downright prose and verse that was neither prose nor verse," sought refuge once again in the polished symmetry and cadence of the rhyming couplet.—THE AUTHOR.

THE VISION OF DANTE.

HELL.

I.

About the time of mortal life's midway,
There roamed in spirit from the truth astray
Forlorn and helpless like a wandering child,
A Cacciaguidan, through a forest wild,
Checked by the valley's growth, torn by the brier.
He finds a slope and longs to clamber higher
For in the vale the shades portend the night
While Phœbus on the mount still lingers bright.
Thus, glad to leave the woods where shadows creep,
He searches for a pathway up the sunlit steep.

II.

In his heart's deep, appalling fear had lain
And weary he and racked with toil and pain,
So dense the gloom he pitiful had passed,
He joys indeed to find escape at last.
Yet short of breath, still with fatigue oppressed,
He turns and views the jungle deep recess'd,
As the beached sailor, rescued from the wave,
Stands and surveys what nearly was his grave,
Then inland wends; so Dante now takes hope,
Moves from the forest gloom and starts to climb the
    slope.

THE GREAT POETS OF ITALY.

III.

But three wild beasts obstruct the mountain pass,
First, panther Florence doth the way harass,
Then Charles of Valois, France's Emperor proud,
In form a lion with his roaring loud,
And lastly, fiercer, hungrier than this,
In she-wolf garb looms deadly Avarice,
The curse of Curian Rome. In deep despair
The pilgrim bard can see no progress there
Till Virgil comes and points another way
Until the conquering greyhound* shall the she-wolf
    slay.

IV.

He who in fable days departed long
Had gained renown, the Roman prince of song,
The bard who immortality had won
In singing of Anchises' worthy son,
The gentle Mantuan, comes from Limbo's realm
To help the pilgrim all his foes o'erwhelm,
To point him o'er the steep and rugged way
Till Hell's dark night should end in Heaven's day,
To stay through demon torments by his side,
Implored by sainted Beatrice to be his guide.

* Supposed to refer to the liberal Veronese, Can Grande della Scala.

THE VISION OF DANTE.

V.

Now is approached the lofty arch of Hell
Where words inscribed of " Hope Abandoned," tell
Where groans and lamentations floating far,
Brood o'er that dark where gleams no cheering star.
These utter forth the never-ending woes
Of those who, nor th' Almighty nor his foes
Could please, among them weakly Celestine
Whom fear his sceptre prompted to resign.
These, hornets sting, and from them tears and blood
Trickle to feed gaunt worms who clustered where they
        stood.

VI.

See Charon with his bark draw nigh to take
The souls condemned across the livid lake!
They who beneath God's anger hapless fell,
Now sentenced in eternal dark to dwell.
He, with his eyes of fire, collects them all,
Wailing, yet heeding close his ghastly call.
No sooner lands he on the farther shore
His piteous cargo, than he comes for more.
Thus the old boatman stern and fierce and rude
Continuous bears to darkness Adam's evil brood.

THE GREAT POETS OF ITALY.

VII.

And next to Limbo, Hell's first circle borne,
That deep abyss they hear with rumblings torn,
The sighs and murmurings of lost souls whose grief
Rather than torture tells of unbelief;
Who lived of old, who had no Gospel light
To teach them how to serve their God aright.
And Virgil, that he sojourns here, reminds,
And noble Homer here the traveller finds,
And Socrates and Plato, too, he sees
With Euclid, Linus, Tully and Diogenes.

VIII.

And many another shade of mighty worth
Which yet from Limbo never could go forth.
These worthy ones, in spite of their disgrace,
Here hold above the throng an honoured place.
And here, the bard is told, had Adam stayed,
And Noah in the realms of darkness strayed.
Here Moses, Abram and King David dwelt;
Here gloom Erebian Israel's sons had felt.
Till these for faith and worthy lives the Son
To bliss exalted and for each a pardon won.

THE VISION OF DANTE.

IX.

And ere the travellers leave Inferno's gate
What further piteous scenes their eyes await—
Of neutral spirits whose indifferent ways
Make them unworthy infamy or praise,
Sharing their grief near the wide Acheron
With careless angels whose last hope is gone,
The unbaptized, despairing and perplexed,
They pass, and still descending, enter next
Where Minos stands to judge each criminal round,
And where those faithless to their wedded vows are
       found.

X.

These, though least blamed of all the sinners lost,
In a great whirlwind constantly are tossed.
Here Helen and Paris, driv'n by cruel winds,
Are seen in anguish; here the poet finds
The fair Francesca, daughter of his friend,
Who storm swept, shares her loved Paolo's end.
And now the gluttons' stinking fate is seen,
Huge rolling weights crush prodigal and mean,
And steered by Phlegyas 'cross the Stygian mire
Is met the drenched Argenti, fallen 'neath anger's fire.

THE GREAT POETS OF ITALY.

XI.

The gates of Dis now open wide and moans
Uberti in his tomb of fire, and groans
Heretic Cavalcanti for his son
Yet soon to his hot grave again sinks down.
Then is the seventh circle reached, that rent
With shrieks and torments of the violent
Tyrants and homicides and thieves who stood
Neck deep in rushing streams of boiling blood.
Attila, Alexander, D'Este here!
While the great plundering Rieneri fill the rear.

XII.

The centaur Nessus guides, and now accursed
The suicides are met, their fate the worst,
Converted into gnarled yet feeling trees,
The carrion harpies feed and glut on these.
Now Capaneus, punished for his pride,
Is found where raining tongues of fire abide,
And scourged Brunetto in the usurers' place,
Whom Dante, loving, lingers to embrace
And tell his old instructor that 'twas he
Who taught how man might merit immortality!

THE VISION OF DANTE.

XIII.

Now mount they Geryon* of terrific mien,
And lowered by him, Hell's circle eight is seen,
The procurers and adulators first,
These scourged, those in most loathsome filth
    immersed.
Next they who barter offices for gain
And simony and soothsaying maintain,
Welter in boiling pitch, have living coals
Eternal burning on their upturned soles,
Or, with heads backward on their bodies, wring
Grief from the passing bard at each distorted thing.

XIV.

Behold the hypocrites in golden dress,
Outwardly gay but weighed with weariness,
For that bright bonnet on each shining head
Crushes its wearer with its load of lead.
And he who counselled that The Christ should die,†
Here on a trampled cross doth abject lie.
And thieves are changed to serpents, yet again
Their viper shapes assume the form of men,
And in hot cloaks of close-confining fire
Those who had counselled fraud find unconsumed
    attire.

---

* The personification of the Monster Fraud.
† Caiaphus, the High Priest.

THE GREAT POETS OF ITALY.

XV.

The tortures of another gulf proclaimed
The heretics and scandal sowers maimed,
All hewn and gashed, these bleeding ones are viewed,
With severed limbs and entrails that protrude.
Here is the poet's heart with sorrow torn
To see the Provençal Bertrand de Born
Bear in his hand with grief, his dripping head,
Disjoined and from its body severèd,
The fate of him who, cruelest of men,
Had set at mutual war the sire and son of Guienne.*

XVI.

Horrid Malebolge! in thee too are heard
The falsifiers in person, act and word,
Some cry with dropsy's disproportioning pains,
Others with fever parching skin and veins.
The shameless Myrrha, who her sire decoyed,†
And she who all her charming wiles employed
To tempt chaste Joseph, Adamo, who made
Base coin and Sinon, he who Troy betrayed.
These last engaging in contention fierce
With wrangling snarls and gibes the lazar regions
     pierce.

---

* Henry II of England and his son John.
† Ovid. met. Lib. 10.

THE VISION OF DANTE.

XVII.

And in thee too is Jason tortured, he
Who drew from virtue fair Hypsipyle
And Fifth Pope Nicholas who when he trod
Earth's pathway trafficked in the things of God,
And Grifolino, he for alchemy
Condemned to suffer loathsome leprosy,
With Siennese Cappocchio bitter wails,
As each in anguish tears his itching scales;
And in thee demons shout and curse and grin
As standing o'er each wretch they plunge the flesh
      hooks in.

XVIII.

Now Nimrod through whom tongue-confusion throve
And Giant Strivers 'gainst almighty Jove
They pass, and are by Antæus lowered till
They reach those doomed Hell's harshest pit to fill,
A vasty circle of four spheres enlaid
In ice to bind the monsters who betrayed
Their relatives, their country or their friends,
And here the vision of Hell's torments ends
Nor can we wonder that the poet feels
No sorrow now, but his kind heart 'gainst pity steels.

THE GREAT POETS OF ITALY.

XIX.

For here in frozen tears, he gazing sees
His own base Florentine contemporaries,
So frigid bound along the icy sweep
Their very weeping suffers not to weep,
And Lucifer besmeared with foam and gore
Reigning unchallenged o'er these regions frore,
He bat-winged and three-headed, feeds upon
The Arch-Betrayer of th' Eternal Son,
And Brutus by whom mighty Cæsar died,
With Cassius shares the judgment of the regicide.

XX.

And pleading through his icy veil of tears,
The friar Alberigo, whose earthly years
Not done, had been to Ptolomea sent
To swifter meet th' assassin's punishment,*
Yet Ugolino, whom Ruggieri slew,
Here from our bard a sigh of pity drew
For his poor sons immersed in famine's tower
All guiltless starved by priestly Pisan power,
But lo! even here were retribution's laws,
For on the prelate skull the victim tireless gnaws.

* He summoned some of his brotherhood with whom he had quar-
relled, to a banquet, under the pretense of reconciliation, and at a
given signal at dessert, assassins rushed in and exterminated all the
guests.

THE VISION OF DANTE.

XXI.

O cursed Cocytus! in whose frozen sphere
Those ice-bound souls in varied forms appear,
In whose hard waves, by wings of Satan fann'd,
The vilest ones encrusted, lean or stand,
Thou well wert chosen as the fittest place
For those whom Dante strove to most disgrace,
Who dwelt on earth their talents to misuse,
Whose crimes the fiends themselves could not excuse.
What agonies are here! What woes condign!
And all the other pangs of Hell are mild to thine.

THE GREAT POETS OF ITALY.

PURGATORY.

I.

HELL left behind and reared on Satan's thigh,
The travellers now emerge and view the sky
And drink the purer air of that new land
Which Cato guards, and resting on its strand,
(For still 'tis dark), wait for the coming light,
Cheered by that cross that charms the southern night.
But soon the shades of darkness flee away
And all around there spreads the dawning day,
And washed by dew of hell's impurities
The bards behold the trembling of the far-off seas.

II.

And Cato wills that they may enter in
And pass those seven rounds where deadly sin
Is purged. And lo! beneath the cleansing hill
A whiteness and a glory shine that fill
The sea with splendour. 'Tis the Bird of God
Guiding the spirits o'er the mystic flood.
These Israel's freedom sing in joyous lay
Then landing o'er the mount enquire the way,
And all, (till Cato chides them,) linger long,
Charmed by the Florentine Casella's matchless song.

THE VISION OF DANTE.

III.

Ere Dante sees the purgatorial gate
He meets a troop, the Excommunicate,
And further on along the steep ascent
The slothful souls and they who late repent,
Manfredi, who had contumacious died,
Belacqua, who in life the harp strings plied,
And lonely Pia of the Siennese,
And Cassero and Montefeltro, these
In turn implore the bard and piteous urge
That intercessions rise their grievous sins to purge.

IV.

And now Sordello's comely shade they meet,
Who reverent grasps his fellow Mantuan's feet
And sadly hears the ancient poet tell
How he a pagan must in Limbo dwell,
He having heard his countryman's weird tale,
Night falling, leads them to a sheltering vale.
Clothed in fair greenery, here they tired stay,
Where a great host of careless rulers pray,
Among them Philip, Rudolph, Ottocar,
And two King Henrys, they of England and Navarre.

THE GREAT POETS OF ITALY.

V.

Here Nino's spirit speaks, the night is spent
And Malaspina predicts banishment.
But as there breaks the radiance of the morn
On Lucia's eagle wings is Dante born
Upmounting to the purgatorial gate
Where Virgil gone before, already sate.
Here three steps lead, and on the last to guard
The Angel of Contrition with his sword,
Who brands upon the poet's brow each sin
And then unlocks the gate and lets the pilgrims in.

VI.

And while their feet across the portal trod
There swelled melodious praise to Heaven's God.
And here perchance befits me to recount
The seven circles of the purging mount:
First there are seen climbing its rocky side
The souls who expiate the sin of pride,
For these beneath a weight of crushing stone
Humility's fair angel tries t' atone;
Next, clad in sackcloth, see poor Sapia rowed
Among the envious with each eyelid tightly sewed.

THE VISION OF DANTE.

VII.

And Duca and Calboli weeping through
Their wired impalements dreadful pictures drew
Of Romagna's and Arno's fallen race,
Once noble, now degenerate and base.
Leaving the round where only closed eyes weep,
They, angel-guarded, climb a further steep
Shrouded in mist, to hear more spirits pray
For peace and wrath's due expiation pay,
Here Lombardo deplores the evil hour
When first there joined the kingly and the papal power.

VIII.

And to another circle clambering still
They see the cleansing of indifference ill,
Where round a beetling rock are sorely press'd
Sloth's victims made to run and never rest;
And next the round where greed of wealth and gold
Is washed away, the pilgrims both behold
These duped ones with the wasters downward keep
Their faces and in deep contrition weep,
Among them Adrian, whose repentant tears
Atone for all the avarice of his earthly years.

245

THE GREAT POETS OF ITALY.

IX.

And now while Capet's spirit utterance
Is making 'gainst the Royal house of France,
The mountain trembles and the startled air
Hears " Gloria in Excelsis " everywhere,
Announcing that from its desire to sin
Some soul is freed and doth its guerdon win.
Statius, the shade whose purging now doth end
And joyous comes to embrace his Mantuan friend,
From hence the Theban poet with them stays
And guides and counsels 'long the purgatorial ways.

X.

A pagan born, to Statius first sufficed
The pagan worship, but there came the Christ
And he embracing firm the true belief,
Domitian's rage and persecution's grief
Had helped to share but only secretly,
For fear compelled and still conforming, he
A pagan outward lived. This cowardly crime
Had earned for him a tedious purging time;
For lukewarmness four cycles here he'd passed,
But now the angels sing his pardon won at last.

THE VISION OF DANTE.

XI.

Poor starved Forese with wan and sunken eye,
Atoning for the sin of gluttony,
Now intercepts the travellers on their way,
Embracing the occasion to inveigh
Against the flaunting open shamelessness
Of his immodest countrywomen's dress,
The bosom bare, the all-uncovered limb,
How bold and unbecoming these to him!
Who here still lingered though his purging years
Had been much shortened by his Nella's prayers and
      tears.

XII.

While he predicts in language accurate
Corso Donati's violent end and fate,
Lo, two fair trees aloft their foliage shoot,
This bearing greed's, that temperance's fruit.
And soon is reached the seventh and final ledge
Where cleansing fire redeems the broken pledge
Of the incontinent, a mighty host
In thirst's consuming torture tried and toss'd,
And, just as day is sinking into night,
An angel points them forward to the topmost height.

THE GREAT POETS OF ITALY.

XIII.

But mark! the man of God demands that first
Must Dante in the fire be immersed
And Virgil tells that to be wholly clean
He must endure the flame, for still between
Himself and Beatrice a wall doth stand
Which fire alone can fell. At this command
He plunges in and lo! the flaming shore
Hears the refrain " Blest they whose hearts are pure."
And Arnault the Provençal, doomed to pay
The price of lust, with Guido greets him on the way.

XIV.

Night falls, of active Leah's meads and streams
And Rachel, deep in thought, the poet dreams,
And now the fires which cleanse the faithless through
The Mantuan shade bids Dante fond adieu.
His guide o'er steeper ways and greater stress
Now leaves him to himself to face the less,
And as the sun proclaims the morning hours
He finds him close to Eden's beauteous bowers
And sees fair bloom and birds of varied wings
And 'cross a limpid rill Matilda joyous sings.

248

THE VISION OF DANTE.

XV.

She, saintly Tuscan Duchess, points afar
To an approaching lustrous heavenly car*
Drawn by a gryphon, emblem of the Christ
With maiden, elder and evangelist
Full manned, and which upon the farther sward
Of Lethe halts close to the awe-struck bard,
And while from the Empyrean overhead
Upon the chariot bloom was scattered,
A green-robed virgin from the fragrance came,
Shedding a hidden virtue clothed in living flame.

XVI.

Beatrice the blest! the dazzling form is hers,
Surrounded by her heavenly quiristers,
She first on him with visage stern doth look
And cruel utters sarcasm's cold rebuke,
" Why, fickle Dante, didst thou ever stray
To earth's deceits from heaven's holier way?
Thou canst not for thy sins approach me here,
Without avowal and repentant tear.
Dost thou these grievous failings full confess?"
The crying, pardon-seeking suppliant falters " Yes."

---

* The Christian Church.

THE GREAT POETS OF ITALY.

XVII.

She further chides, reminding how he fell
When she had left terrestrial scenes to dwell
Above. But watch the contrite sinner sink
To earth and over him at Lethe's brink
Matilda stoop and draw him through the tide
And safely land upon the other side,
With sin's remembrance wholly washed away,
To hear the heav'nly nymphs to Beatrice pray,
Her second beauty to him just immerst
T' unveil and quench the suppliant's ten years' burning
      thirst.

XVIII.

Now risen from the Lethan waters, he
Hears angels chanting " Tu Asperges Me."
The heavenly concourse moving sees arise
A mighty tree upbranching to the skies.*
The tree and car Jove's dreadful lightning licks;
A fox, the treachery of heretics,
Jumps on the car his hunger to appease;
An eagle spreads his feathers over,† these
Scarce happen when a dragon from beneath‡
Tears at the chariot's bottom with his ravenous teeth.

---

* The Roman Empire.
† The gifts of Constantine.
‡ Mahomet.

THE VISION OF DANTE.

XIX.

And perched beyond th' assemblage far above
A harlot* and a giant huge† make love.
But now at saintly Beatrice' command
Matilda takes the pilgrims by the hand
And Tuscan bard and Theban disappear
In Eunoe's reviving waters clear,
Which, rising from a common fountain source,
With Lethe now pursue an adverse course,
And serve a different purpose, bring again
Remembrance of forgotten virtues back to men.

XX.

Thus was our poet tried, thus stern reproved
By her who, while reproving still had loved,
And having passed in deep humility
Before the lustrous car, the towering tree
To him that veilèd beauty long concealed
Of his adored, was now in full revealed,
Washed by those streams which sins eliminate
And thoughts of virtuous deeds anew create.
His burdens left behind, his faults forgiven,
He soars with his beloved and with her enters Heaven.

---

* The Church degraded by Boniface VIII.
† Philip IV of France.

THE GREAT POETS OF ITALY.

PARADISE.

I.

To those celestial, bright, untravelled spheres
They now are borne where, wafted on the ears,
Come harmonies so faultless, so benign
They hold the very ear of the Divine.
On lightning wings they sweep the universe,
Viewing each heavenly planet in their course,
These in alignment so complete, unflaw'd
As to portray their great Creator, God:
And humbly doth the transformed bard confess
How poor are human words to paint such loveliness.

II.

By that magnetic force 'yond man's control,
Which draws above the freed yet yearning soul,
They circle through a fiery realm and soon
Are in the pearly heaven of the moon,
And as they gazed, pale faces at them smiled,
Whom failure of their vows had here exiled,
Yet happy these, nor striving to aspire
To more exalted state or heaven higher,
For now they from ambition find release
And in the Will of Him Who placed them here, their
     peace.

THE VISION OF DANTE.

III.

'Mong these were Piccarda, whom Corso bore
From cloistered walls, and from whose body tore
The sacred vestments; royal Constance too,
By force constrained the nunnery to eschew.
"Is it," the poet asks, "quite just and fair
That these the lesser joys of heaven must share,
With intent of the best, yet backward thrown
By violence nor choosing of their own?"
His guide replies: "These kept the earthly track
And obdurate, did not, though they might have hast-
     ened back."

IV.

Now to that region* whose soft soothing light
The sun inferior makes by beams more bright,
Known as the second heaven, their journey ran,
Where dwelt the soul of great Justinian,
Whose fame the other Cæsars overawes,
In that he gave the Romans better laws.
He Rome's vast feats and victories reviews,
Alludes in passing to the guilty Jews
And how for man was won on Calvary's Hill
Th' atoning priceless gift of liberty of will.

---

* Mercury.

253

THE GREAT POETS OF ITALY.

V.

Then to bright Venus, Star of perfect love!
They glide from shaded Mercury above.
That glorious orb to whom the ancients paid
Their vows and humblest invocations made;
Part of the year effulgent in the night,
The other part a morning satellite.
Here dwelt the soul of Hungary's Martel,
Whom Dante loved in life surpassing well,
Who points out to the two how often are
The destinies of men directed by a Star.

VI.

And Dante marvels and esteems it queer
That amorous Cunizza should be here,
Sister to Romana's base lord, who stood
In Hell's detested stream of boiling blood.
But stranger still! here Rahab's ransom'd soul
Most radiant glows, the first of those made whole
By Christ's atonement, and in Venus' heaven
By Virtue's power a queenly order given;
And lustrous and bejewelled shines nearby
Folco, the learned poet-bishop of Marseilles.

THE VISION OF DANTE.

VII.

The glorious sun, of heavens in number four,
The mounting pair exultant now explore.
And entering its seraphic clime there fell
Upon their hearing song ineffable.
Here two bright circles of the glorified
A space distract the poet from his guide,
While Saint Aquinas, chief of school divines,
To just Saint Francis boundless praise assigns,
And tells against parental pressure how
To poverty the good Ascesian gave his vow.

VIII.

In these two rounds, stamped with the scholar's mark,
There shone Constantinople's patriarch.*
Here learning, reared by faith triumphant rode,
Here Anselm dwelt and Isidore abode.
The one God's Being foremost to reveal,†
The other long Archbishop of Seville.
And Bonaventure, 'mid the august train,
Extols the name of Dominic of Spain,
And Solomon, the wise, vouchsafes t' attest
How glorified will be the bodies of the blest.

---

* Saint Chrysostom.

† Many modern writers express the conviction that although Descartes is generally credited with the first demonstration of God's existence the honour really belonged to Anselm several centuries before.

255

THE GREAT POETS OF ITALY.

IX.

Here slain Böetius and Bede appear,
And Nathan, David's fierce accusing seer.
But now their wanderings lift them up to Mars,
The brightest 'mong the galaxy of stars.
Where in a radiant cross were deep inlaid
Like gems, the warriors of the great crusade,
And gentle strains of music captivate,
While to and fro the spirits scintillate.
And lo! from these the martyrs in Christ's war
Speaks forth the Cacciaguidan, Dante's ancestor.

X.

Himself disclosing in this sentence brief
" I am thy root and thou of me the leaf,"
The ancient forebear then proceeds to say
How Florence had degraded since his day
" In leathern girdle plainly dress'd our men
Nor cursed our streets with flaunting women then,
No dowry asked at marriage to exceed
Our means to pay, through grasping bridegroom's
        greed,
Our food was plain, our houses in accord,
And banishment had not oppressed us, nor the sword!"

THE VISION OF DANTE.

XI.

" Sad day it was when Buondelmonte slain,
Peace fled our portals ne'er to reign again,
And sadder still when Florence's fair land
Ambitious rulers struggled to expand,
And with the hordes from Campi and Fighine
To mingle and her own best blood bemean.
Our arms had never then been hung reversed,
Nor through division dyed with gules accursed.
The upstart Adimari were not great,
The noble Ravignani graced Saint Peter's gate."

XII.

" Soon thou, my son, from Florence must depart,
Whom thou dost love with a true patriot's heart,
Driven by thy cruel enemies from home,
Urged by the plots of simonaic Rome.
But Florence shall deplore the day she lent
Her influence to decree thy banishment.
A shelter thou shalt find, a peaceful rest
With fam'd Can Grande, of lords the kindest, best.
A poem thou shalt write, whose withering flame
Shall put the mightiest of thy countrymen to shame."

THE GREAT POETS OF ITALY.

XIII.

He spake, and o'er the sparkling cross there ran
Orlando's dazzling sprite and Charlemagne,
And Joshua and Godfrey, glittering, free,
With Guiscard and the mighty Maccabee,
And other worthy heroes. Now with her,
His heavenly guide, he soars to Jupiter,
Sixth of celestial realms whose silvern light
Clothed those who in the world had ruled aright.
Gem clustered, and in eagle form arrayed,
These as one voice address the poet and the maid.

XIV.

" Ye see me in this height of glory thus,
For I on earth was just and piteous,
And think not 'tis decreed that they are lost
Who die without the sign of baptism cross'd.
Trajan and Ripheus whom ye see are here,
By Faith and Hope and Love attained our sphere,
Invincible with these they Heaven assailed
And o'er the Will of The Most High prevailed.
And in the final judgment sad the fate
Of many a loud, lip-serving, baptized potentate."

THE VISION OF DANTE.

XV.

Of this huge bird six spirits formed the eye,
Of sainted kings revolving lustrously,
Great David in the pupil, arched around
The two unwashed, and Constantine renowned,
And Hezekiah and William named the Good ;*
These six the fires of greatest magnitude.
But now our twain repair to that far heaven,
Among the blessed realms in number seven,
Where rose a golden ladder of such height
The upper part was misted from their gazing sight.

XVI.

On Saturn's rungs as they in rays descend
The spirits of the Contemplative blend
In splendour multitudinous.   A sprite
Speaks forth from these, 'tis Damiano's light,
The monk of Catria who in life had checked
And striven the priestly evils to correct.
He warns: " Predestination's theme is such
That even the very angels dare not touch,"
Tells how he once had donned the scarlet hat
And paints the modern prelate indolent and fat.

---

* William II, King of Sicily.

THE GREAT POETS OF ITALY.

XVII.

Soon as that saint,* who at Cassino broke
The pagan idols, had appeared and spoke
Against the monks' impurities and sins,
They reach the Constellation of the Twins,
The Starry Sphere, of heavens numbered eight,
And from its lofty summit contemplate
The universe beneath, our little world,
And all the astral host around unfurl'd,
Mercury and Venus, Saturn, Jove, the Moon,
Mars and the shining offspring of Hyperion.†

XVIII.

But mark! still brighter beams do now entrance
For lo! there glows the Christly Radiance!
The Virgin Mother's heavenly form attends
A countless train of spirits blest descends,
While circling Son and Sainted Mother, fell
Depicting Angel Love, Saint Gabriel.
Spellbound, the poet looks, enraptured, he
Loses his mortal in infinity,
As high The Virgin's praise melodious rang
And all the glorified " Regina Coeli " sang.

* St. Benedict.
† The sun.

THE VISION OF DANTE.

XIX.

Now Dante's faith is tested, questions given
By Cephas, holder of the keys of Heaven.
The answers meet, again upon him waits
Saint James, who on Hope's joys interrogates;
Next comes, his knowledge of pure Love to weigh,
He who upon The Saviour's bosom lay.
Then Adam's light shines forth and deigns to tell
How he in Eden placed, transgressing, fell,
His length of years on earth and what his tongue
And when and how the seraph throng he came among.

XX.

A sudden change! all round behold the sky
Eclipse and alter to a vermeil dye.
They hear Saint Peter tell of the disgrace
Heaped on his Church by carnal Boniface;
How Popes their seal on war and strife bestow,
How wolves devour the shepherd fold below.
Then mount to that swift circle, number nine,
Where nought may dwell except the souls divine,
Where time's deep roots begin their journeyings
And motion for the spheres in its vast order springs.

THE GREAT POETS OF ITALY.

XXI.

Here round the Godly Essence burning bright
Revolve in wingèd song the choirs of light,
Nine chanting hosts, three saintly hierarchies
Of Domination, Virtue, Power, these
In motion of the wheels of earth reversed,
Those outside last, those next the Godhead first.
" My charge, thou now must know that happiness
In seeing more than loving finds excess,"
His guide exclaims and then in scorn inveighs
'Gainst the unworthy theologians of those days.

XXII.

To the last heaven, the vast Empyrean bright,
Of incorporeal, unembodied light,
Now Beatrice leads, in semblance to a rose,
Where more than million saints on thrones repose,
And spirits of both orders Old and New
Disport among its perfumed petals' dew,
Clustering and swarming like the honey bees,
Amid infinitude of fragrancies.
But now ascends her well-won throne, his guide,
And Bernard, Clairvaux' abbot, hastens to his side.

THE VISION OF DANTE.

XXIII.

Now many sainted women pass in view,
Of the Old Hebrew Law and of the New,
And patriarch and martyr spirits shone,
Moses with those, with these beheaded John;
And Bernard tells how each has here a place,
Not by his merit only, but by grace.
Then points he out The Mother's face benign,
Seen high above The Lustrous Host to shine,
And urges Dante if her grace he'd share
He must The Heavenly Virgin supplicate in prayer.

XXIV.

He prays! nor does the suppliant ask in vain,
She heeds! and, nearest throned to the Arcane,
Casts on the praying one her loving sight
And pleads for him The Eternal Sovereign Light.
And lo! at length 'tis given to him to see
The unveiled Glory of the Trinity;
To view those sights to human eye obscured,
To hear those sounds no mortal ear hath heard;
His knowledge widens as he looks above
And deep, beyond the measure of the world, his love!

FINIS.

GENERAL INDEX

OF

AUTHORS, CHARACTERS, PLACES AND EVENTS
MENTIONED OR REFERRED TO
IN THIS VOLUME.

INDEX.

INDEX.

INDEX.

INDEX.

INDEX.

INDEX.

271

INDEX.

INDEX.

INDEX.

INDEX.

INDEX.

INDEX.

INDEX.

INDEX.

INDEX.

INDEX.

INDEX.

INDEX.

NOTE.—It will be observed in this index that in treating the Italian poets comparison, criticism or reference has been made as well to no less than fifty-four of the English poets.

CPSIA information can be obtained at www.ICGtesting.com
Printed in the USA
LVOW091754060613

337354LV00013B/502/P